Presented To:

_____

From:

_____

Date:

_____

The POWER *of the*
ORIGINAL
CHURCH

The POWER *of the* ORIGINAL CHURCH

Turning the World Upside Down

JOSEPH L. GREEN JR.

DESTINY IMAGE® PUBLISHERS, INC.

P.O. Box 310, Shippensburg, PA 17257-0310

"Speaking to the Purposes of God for This Generation and for the Generations to Come."

This book and all other Destiny Image, Revival Press, MercyPlace, Fresh Bread, Destiny Image Fiction, and Treasure House books are available at Christian bookstores and distributors worldwide.

For a U.S. bookstore nearest you, call 1-800-722-6774.

For more information on foreign distributors, call 717-532-3040.

Reach us on the Internet: www.destinyimage.com.

ISBN 13 TP: 978-0-7684-3755-3
ISBN 13 Ebook: 978-0-7684-9004-6

For Worldwide Distribution, Printed in the U.S.A.

1 2 3 4 5 6 7 8 9 10 /15 14 13 12 11

ENDORSEMENTS

The truth that is so carefully revealed to us in this book is not only powerful, but accurate. Pastor Joe Green has searched the Scriptures and makes an extremely relevant case that today's Church would be wise to adhere to. This book is not just a must for your library; it's a must for the Body of Christ!

LARRY A. COLBERT
CEO Lael Music Group
www.larrycolbertmusic.com, www.ksongz.com
www.memorialsong.net

It's time for the Bride of Christ to operate in the fullness of the dunamis power that God has made available to us. In *The Original Church,* Pastor Joseph L. Green, challenges the Church at large to set aside every weight that would hinder us from being about our Father's Kingdom business with fervent, urgent potency. This challenging, thought-provoking text will prompt even seasoned believers to question their long-held assumptions. Read it and prepare for a power surge!

DR. KENYA F. AYERS
Host, *Prescriptions for Hope with Dr. Kenya,*
WEXL & WMUZ radio
Executive Director, Esperanza Communications

This book is a true read everyone should take to heart! It is written by a greatly beloved, righteous pastor who sees and hears clearly from God. Pastor Joe is a chosen vessel and a man of preciousness.

MINISTER JUDY KEEFER
Mechanicsburg, PA

I'm so glad God gave Pastor Joe the vision to write this book. I learned a lot of things about different Bible versions. I never knew about the pagan holidays I thought were holy and the true history behind them. What are the true days we should honor God with His celebrating? It's all in this book. You can tell Pastor Joe put his heart and soul into this book by the thorough research he did. He had a lot of facts to back him up, with the Word of God being the main one. Thank you, Pastor Joe, for enlightening me. I'm proud to call you friend.

HARRY C. GRACE
Harrisburg, PA

The Original Church is a fascinating look at the Church that will hopefully inspire the people of God to rise up and claim their rightful place in the world and the Kingdom of God. Joseph Green delves deep into the Church's past with a detailed and scholarly eye, bringing to light some of the Church's true history that has regrettably been lost to much of today's generation. A truly enlightening and eye-opening read. I highly recommend this book.

DANIEL FAZZINA
Co-Creator/Host, *Divine Intervention* radio show
Author, *Divine Intervention: Amazing True Stories of
God's Miracles Today—Volume I*

TABLE OF CONTENTS

PREFACE

Wow! Thank You, Jesus! This book is *so* powerful and factual! We learned so much from it. It is an eye-opener, absolutely dynamic, and totally in line with the Word of God. When this book is read and adhered to, God will indeed use *this Church on Earth now to turn the world upside down!*

God blessed us to be present when Pastor Joe was ordained as "Pastor to the Nations." We knew then that he would be traveling, but now realize that the message that God has given him is *for the nations.* He cannot reach each person in person, but the message that God has given him is *for each person of every nation!*

We know that God has placed gifts in the Church, in the Body of Christ. This book should be required reading for every one of those gifts, for every pastor, evangelist, teacher, prophet, and apostle, so that the Holy Spirit can use them to minister the "right way"—God's Way of doing things to the Body of Christ in these last days.

Our personal testimony is that the Holy Spirit has led us to observe the Feast Days and God's ordinances for the past two years. As we learned more about God's Word and satan's lies, we were obligated to choose life or death. We chose life! We love Jesus, so we are learning to keep His commands. As we keep God's commands, we continuously watch God's blessings overtake us more than we could have ever have imagined! He will never change, so we must! *His way* is great!

Our background was Baptist, Pentecostal, and Catholic. We are born-again Christians, according to the Word of God, but we had to awaken out of sleep, stop allowing satan to deceive us, stop being religious, stop participating in anti-Christ holidays, stop eating certain foods, and begin to let the Kingdom of God rule and reign in and through us. In other words, we had to let Jesus Christ be Lord of all— including the days we observe and foods we eat; we need to obey His Word and stop compromising it!

During the last two years, it was a blessing for us to learn that God was doing the same thing in Pastor Joe. *God wishes that we prosper and be in health, even as our souls prosper* (see 3 John 2).

As Pastor Joe says in this dynamic book, "In order to truly please God, our first step is obedience to His Word." And, "Obedience comes first and then revelation from God follows." *Amen! So be it!*

Thank you our dear brother and friend, Pastor Joe, Pastor to the Nations, for being obedient to the Holy Ghost as He drew you to learn of Him and His Way of doing things. God shall use what you have written to change multitudes of lives in all nations of the world to walk in the way, the truth, and the life.

The timing of this book is perfect; it should be in the hands of every believer and should be read and reread over and over again! It will help all of the readers and doers to walk in the fullness of the blessing of the Gospel of Jesus Christ, to walk in demonstration and power of the Holy Ghost, and most of all, to be rapture-ready!

Love and Shalom,
REV. MICHAEL and REV. DR. SHIRLEY KNOTHE
Co-Pastors, Perfectly Whole Christian Center

THE POWER OF THE ORIGINAL CHURCH

By Don Nori Sr.

I was swept into the faith back in the tumultuous days of the Vietnam War, the Flower Child movement of hippies, drugs, race riots, anarchy, and fear. Little did I know that what was called the Church was fast asleep, with little understanding of the events of the day or of what God was about to do, completely in His own sovereignty.

The nation was awash with turmoil on every level of society, culture, religion, and government. The long, hot summers of the mid-1960s spilled into the growing stress of the anti-war protests, assassinations, sexual revolution, and the general breakdown of cultural morality.

That set the stage for the restoration of God's Presence and purposes in the Earth to an extent that we had not seen for over 100 years. People once again discovered God's love. They experienced God's power and enjoyed His Presence in unprecedented ways. Unfortunately, human nature being what it is, much of the progress made concerning the Church Jesus is building stalled in the malaise of personal ambition and the grab for power and control.

Today, as a society, we are in even more difficult times than we were in the 1960s. Our children are in serious confusion. The attacks on our way of life from within and without are relentless at best. Global unrest has not yet peaked as economic uncertainty keeps many unable to cope. Terror is a constant concern as humanity is facing threats that could radically and forever change our way of living. *But God...*

Everything is changing. This is a simple fact. Church as we know it is over. For the Church Jesus is building does not ignore the pain and suffering, hopelessness and despair of a crumbling world. Unless our faith is touching the world around us, it is a non-functioning faith. Jesus lived to bring the rule of God to this planet, and His Church is the vehicle that will bring it to pass. One does not have to be a prophet to see that the Holy Spirit is moving within believers in search of those who covet reality in relationships, faith, and personal destiny. While religion has made the words of believers sound hollow and ineffective, God has been and is at work in His people to bring wholeness and love to the masses.

When the Bible was first made available to the common person so many centuries ago, it sparked a revolution of creativity, thought, hope, love, and wealth. Absolutely everything changed as a result of this release of God's Word. There is no doubt that such a release of new creativity, opportunity, relationship, and the miraculous is on the horizon. Most important is the return of the Priesthood that belongs to every believer. Heaven is poised to pour out unprecedented power and life. The reason for this 21st-century global spiritual awakening is much the same thing that sparked the Renaissance. The release of God's Word, this time in the hearts of hungry believers who are no longer satisfied with Christianity as it has been practiced over many centuries, will redefine everything.

"Church" as we have come to know it is most certainly in the cross hairs of the explosion of life and power. The Church Jesus is building is finally defining truth in light of reality, relationship, and experience.

And it needs to be this way. For too many folk have become accustomed to defining *Church* by what is, thus changing what the normal Christian experience was in the early days of the Church's existence. It has become too easy to explain away the lack of power and Presence in the Church with obscure doctrine developed with interpretational latitude that would cause Paul himself roll over in his grave.

It is far more intellectually and spiritually correct to return to what was always seen as the focal point of the believers' fellowship and conversation and was, indeed, the very reason for their coming together—the manifest Presence of the Lord in the midst of their meetings. That was, of course, God's love emboldened by His power and divine authority. The Church Jesus is building is a Church of power, wonder, hope, healing, and restoration. This is the Church we seek, the Church we love, the Church that He, Himself is building.

Therefore, it is of absolute importance that books like this begin to fill the hearts and minds of all who seek Him in truth that is based in reality. The study of what *was* in order to rediscover what *is now needed* to return to the supernatural, normal Christian life will undoubtedly reignite the flame of divine reality in our hearts and move us ever closer to God's original intention for humanity—that He would have a people for His own possession, demonstrating the Kingdom of Heaven right here on this planet.

INTRODUCTION

This book is the culmination of a very interesting journey. God has a way of setting up situations and circumstances that cause us to do what He wants us to do. If He were to just tell us to do things we would probably do them incorrectly; we would put them off, or we would simply not do them at all. Because of His infinite wisdom, He orders our steps to cause us to do His will. He knows what buttons to push and when to push them, He knows the things that motivate us, and He knows how much pressure to apply on us to shape us into what we need to be for His purposes. Romans chapter 8 shows us that all things work together for good for those who are called according to His purpose (see Rom. 8:28).

I want to first let you know that I am not a formally trained theologian. I do not have a university degree in theology, nor have I attended a traditional seminary; my college degree is in communications. I used to think that this would discount a person from taking on an endeavor like this one, but the Lord showed me that the apostle Paul dealt with a similar issue. Paul was very well-trained as a theologian and had the equivalent of a doctorate in theology. He bragged about being trained by Gamaliel, a Pharisee who was regarded as one of the greatest biblical teachers of his day. Paul then went on to show that although he had received the finest teaching people had to offer, he had not fully under-stood what the Holy Scriptures said concerning the Messiah.

I am not by any means knocking a formal Bible education. What I have found is that only through a true revelation from God can we fully understand the things of God. Paul wrote in the Book of Galatians that the Gospel that he preached did not come from people, but from Jesus Himself. We all need a revelation from God about what He is saying through His Word.

The unique thing about this book is that it is a layperson's journey into a deep biblical study. Anyone who has a desire can learn to rightly divide the Word of truth (see 2 Tim. 2:15). God is a rewarder of all who dili-gently seek Him (see Heb. 11:6). I lay out my position and then provide the resources that will allow you to take the journey with me.

My journey started while I was doing a daily radio show. I used to give a daily question called the "Bible knowledge question" on the show. I had to change the title because it was first called "Bible trivia," but one of the elders informed me that there was nothing trivial about the Word of God. I totally agree. At the time I had a parallel Bible that contained four translations side by side. The translations were the King James Version, the Amplified Bible, the New International Version, and the New American Standard Bible. While researching one of the questions for the program, I came across several glaring differences between the translations. This started me on the journey that brought me to Section III of this book, discussing how the enemy has changed the Word of God.

During this time, I was invited to a Messianic Passover meal with a local Messianic congregation that had a radio program on the station. Being raised in a Baptist church, I had never even heard of a Passover "seder." As I sat at the meal and heard the rabbi explain the elements of the Passover, I felt the overwhelming presence of the Holy Spirit. I knew this was truly of God. This experience gave me a passion to find out more about God's "appointed times." I searched the Scriptures to find out where God told us that we were to no longer keep the feasts; I still have not found it. This is why I wrote Section II on how the enemy has changed the "times" of God.

As I stated previously, I do not have a formal theological education. I have, however, spent countless hours studying and researching the things that I have written about in this book. I have studied biblical Hebrew and have spent countless hours under teachings about these topics. I have also included many resources for all of those interested in following the information that I discuss. Even though I don't hold a bachelor's degree, a master's degree, or a doctorate in the Bible, this five-year journey has made me feel as though I do.

This book is a guide to help take you on the wonderful journey that the Lord took me on. This journey has taken me to such a deep understanding of God and His character that I knew I needed to share it with others. As much as I thought I loved and respected the Lord previously, this journey brought me deeper than I ever expected. I pray that it will do the same for you as well.

I have found that a myriad of treasures are locked in the pages of the Bible that most Christians have missed out on, mostly because of tradition and also the spirit of anti-Semitism that has infiltrated the Body of Christ. God is illuminating these deep and beautiful truths so that we can walk in full authority as Kingdom citizens. The first Church experienced a deep relationship with the Messiah, but over time that relationship has been strained through misinterpretation and deception. In this season, the Lord is reconnecting us to the power and authority of the original Church. As God's people, we are meant to be called out and separated to reveal the glory and the power of God.

I challenge you to read this with an open mind. Put away your denominational biases and your preconceived notions of how you relate to God. No matter how long you have been studying the Holy Bible and no matter how deep your relationship with God is, I believe you will discover something more. We can all experience more of God.

Section I

SETTING THE
FOUNDATION

Chapter 1

WHY THE CHURCH HAS
LOST ITS POWER

The purpose for this book is to spell out some of the ways that I believe
God is trying to reenergize His Church. As we get closer to the return
of Jesus Christ, the Church that our Lord is coming back for must be
without spot or wrinkle. He is coming back for a purified Bride who has
a passion and a burning desire for Him—as much as He has for us. The
Holy Spirit is revealing to us how to become the very people for whom
Jesus Christ gave Himself as a living sacrifice.

What God has given us in His Word and what we are actually living
are drastically different. Instead of walking in power, we are walking as a
defeated and powerless Body that does not represent what the Bible says
we should be. We aren't changing our communities, nor are we stirring
up the type of respect and awe that the first Church demanded. Make
no mistake: There is always a "remnant" that God reserves for Himself.
This remnant is walking in the power of God. However, the Church
today—the Body of Christ as a whole—is powerless. The overall Body
of believers who call themselves Christians look nothing like what God
designed. This book will provide some of the keys that I believe we need
to reinsert in order to restore the Church to what God had intended.

JESUS GAVE HIS CHURCH POWER

The first Church moved in the power and authority that Jesus Christ meant for us to have. He gave His disciples an indication of what was to come before He ascended into Heaven.

> *And, being assembled together with them, commanded them that they should not depart from Jerusalem, but wait for the promise of the Father, which, saith He, ye have heard of Me. For John truly baptized with water; but ye shall be baptized with the Holy Ghost not many days hence. When they therefore were come together, they asked of Him, saying, Lord, wilt Thou at this time restore again the kingdom to Israel? And He said unto them, It is not for you to know the times or the seasons, which the Father hath put in His own power. But **ye shall receive power**, after that the Holy Ghost is come upon you: and ye shall be witnesses unto Me both in Jerusalem, and in all Judaea, and in Samaria, and unto the uttermost part of the earth* (Acts 1:4-8).

This power that Jesus talked about not only gave the early apostles a boldness to preach the Gospel, but it also gave them the power that was needed to impact change on their surroundings. The word *power* comes from the Greek word *dunamis* (pronounced *doo'-nam-is*) *which means force* (literally or figuratively); specifically miraculous *power* (usually by implication a *miracle* itself):—ability, abundance, meaning, might (-ily, -y, -y deed), (worker of) miracle (-s), power, strength, violence, mighty (wonderful) work.[1] Jesus was telling His disciples that the power that they were going to receive from the Holy Spirit would give them the ability to do the miraculous.

For the first few hundred years after Jesus' ascension to Heaven, the Church was very different from what we see today. The Church was filled with the power of God. Everywhere the early followers of Jesus went they changed their environment.

> *And when they found them not, they drew Jason and certain brethren unto the rulers of the city, crying, These that have turned the world upside down are come hither also* (Acts 17:6).

THE CHURCH AFTER PENTECOST

On the day of Pentecost, the Holy Spirit fell on 120 people in the city of Jerusalem. By the end of that same day, 3,000 converts were added to the Church. Within a year's time, the Church had more than tripled in size, numbering more than 10,000 people. Historians believe that at the time of Stephen's murder, about two years later, the Church numbered approximately 20,000 people. In spite of great persecution, the early Church continued to grow by leaps and bounds.

One of the greatest examples of this growth was the church in Ephesus. In Acts chapter 19, Paul went to Ephesus and began preaching the Gospel. He resided there for about two years. During this time, the city of Ephesus had a population of about 200,000 people. The churches in Colossae, as well as the seven churches mentioned in the Book of Revelation chapters 2 and 3, were also planted during that time.

The church in Ephesus grew so rapidly that it disrupted the city's economy. The Book of Acts chapter 19 describes a big uproar that took place because Paul had turned large numbers of people away from idol worship.

> *For a certain man named Demetrius, a silversmith, which made silver shrines for Diana, brought no small gain unto the craftsmen; whom he called together with the workmen of like occupation, and said, Sirs, ye know that by this craft we have our wealth. Moreover ye see and hear, that not alone at*

Ephesus, but almost throughout all Asia, this Paul hath per-suaded and turned away much people, saying that they be no gods, which are made with hands (Acts 19:24-26).

When Paul came to preach the Gospel, it changed the environment. Before this, most of the city's residents were pagans who worshiped the goddess Diana. The Holy Spirit fell on the region, and the citizens began worshiping the true and living God. Idol worship no longer satisfied them, and they abandoned their pagan practices. The people who had made a lot of money by selling statues to their residents in the community began to protest. Most of their customers were no longer buying idols to worship. So the local idol makers were very angry at Paul and the Christians who were taking over the community.

I can just imagine a group of people throwing down their idols and anything else that was not in line with the Word of God. They exchanged the lies of the devil and idolatry for a relationship with Jesus Christ. Wouldn't it be great to see a revival like this take place in your town or state? Can you just imagine the drug dealers, the pornographers, the prostitutes, and the murderers turning their lives over to Jesus? I believe it is just as possible today as it was nearly 2,000 years ago.

So that not only this our craft is in danger to be set at nought; but also that the temple of the great goddess Diana should be despised, and her magnificence should be destroyed, whom all Asia and the world worshippeth. And when they heard these sayings, they were full of wrath, and cried out, saying, Great is Diana of the Ephesians. And the whole city was filled with confusion: and having caught Gaius and Aristarchus, men of Macedonia, Paul's companions in travel, they rushed with one accord into the theatre (Acts 19:27-29).

An interesting side note to the story of Diana: Diana was a fertility goddess that was heavily worshiped during the spring festivals in which fertility rites were celebrated. Diana has had many names throughout different times and regions. Another name for the goddess Diana is *Astarte* or *Estre,* which has become part of the Christian-pagan observance of Easter. We will discuss this more coming up.

By the time Paul wrote his first letter to Timothy, around A.D. 63, the church in Ephesus numbered approximately 60,000 people. At the height of the church in Ephesus, the number of members may have been as many as 100,000, about half of the total population of the city. The early Church literally "took the city" for Jesus.

In the year A.D. 112, about 80 years after Pentecost, the Roman author Pliny wrote a letter to Emperor Trajan. In his letter he complained about the province of Asia Minor, where Ephesus was located: "...temples to the pagan gods are almost totally forsaken and Christians are everywhere a multitude."[2]

This pattern was taking place all over the Roman Empire. Tertullian wrote to the pagans in his *Apologia:*

> We have filled every place belonging to you—cities, islands, castles, towns, assemblies, your very camp, your tribes, companies, palace, senate, and forum! We leave you your temples only. We can count your armies; our numbers in a single province will be greater.[3]

THE CHURCH IN THE SECOND AND THIRD CENTURIES

The New Testament Church lived in a constant state of revival lasting hundreds of years. This was a sustained, multi-generational revival. It spread everywhere, and the world could not stand against it! By the end of the first century, the early Church had spread throughout the known world. It extended from India on the east to England on the west and from Germany on the north to Ethiopia on the south. Its expansion amazed the world.

Dr. Robert Heidler writes:

> It was not unusual for a church to be planted in a city and rapidly grow to 20 or 30,000 members. Some historians estimate that by the end of the third century, half the population of the Roman Empire had converted to Christianity. This expansion of the early church took place in the middle of a totally pagan, immoral culture, during the times of severe persecution.[4]

Justin Martyr wrote during the middle of the second century:

> There are no people, Greek or Barbarian, or any other race; by whatsoever appellation or manners they may be distinguished...whether they dwell in tents or wander about in covered wagons...among whom prayers and thanksgivings are not offered in the name of the crucified Christ.[5]

The historian Philip Schaff writes:

> It may be fairly asserted that about the end of the third century the name of Christ was known, revered, and persecuted in every province and every city of the empire....In all probability at the close of the third century the church numbered ten million souls.[6]

Can you imagine how much power the early Church must have had? The apostles went into areas that had been pagan for centuries, and within a few decades the power of God had run roughshod through the most powerful empire on Earth. Add this to the facts that great persecution was taking place and that the first apostles, who had walked with

Christ, had lost their lives spreading the Gospel of Jesus Christ. These facts did nothing to hinder the spread of the truth of Jesus Christ, and many people accepted Him as Lord.

The first Church moved with tremendous power! At the rate that the Church started, the whole world should be proclaiming the name of Christ by now. But something very interesting happened. The question we must ask ourselves is...

WHERE DID THE POWER GO?

When we see the impact that the first Church had for the first 200 to 300 years after the day of Pentecost, we have to question why today's Church as a whole is not putting the modern-day idol makers out of business. In recent times, instead of the Church invading and conquering the kingdom of darkness, we have more often compromised our faith to accommodate the world. We have assimilated the world into the Church more than changing the world by the power that the Church once had.

In 21st-century America in particular, the current state of the Church is not good. We have allowed the world to dictate to us what is right and what is important. The members of our local congregations can be better described as "Christians in Name only." We call ourselves followers of Christ, but are we really living like children of God? Divorce is rampant in our churches. Fornication and adultery are reported just as much in the Church as they are in the world. Neighborhoods where many of our churches are located have extremely high crime rates.

The Church in America is a shell of the original Church. I have many close friends in parts of India and Africa who are truly walking in the power and authority of the original Church. They suffer great persecution, yet have an uncompromising view of their relationship with God. A pastor friend of mine received "stripes" on his back because he was spreading the Gospel. In many parts of India, you are allowed to be a Christian, but you are just not allowed to evangelize. Because of their passion to spread the Gospel of Jesus Christ, they willingly suffer physical beatings rather than compromise.

My friends from Africa walk miles through desert regions to have Christian meetings. They will stay for days, and their prayer lives are second to none. Because of this, they have many miracles demonstrated in their churches. Their passion for the Kingdom of God manifests itself through signs and wonders not seen since the first few hundred years after the day of Pentecost written in Acts chapter 2.

The early Church changed the environment in all the cities where it was located. The people in those places changed their ways to adapt to a life of obedience to God. Heathens didn't dictate policy to the Church; the Church dictated doctrine in the communities. That same power is still available to us right now! Once we have learned to get in sync with God, I believe we will once again rule and reign in the power of Jesus Christ. This book will attempt to offer several keys to reenergize the dying Bride, but first we must look at what happened to cause the decline in the Church's power.

Chapter 2

THE DEVICES OF SATAN

The devil could not have been happy about the power and explosive growth of the early Church. So he planned a strategy to weaken God's Church and retain his power. Being aware of his devices will help us to overcome them.

> *Lest Satan should get an advantage of us: for we are not ignorant of his devices* (2 Corinthians 2:11).

CHANGING TIMES AND LAWS

> *And he shall speak great words against the most High, and shall wear out the saints of the most High, and think to change times and laws: and they shall be given into his hand until a time and times and the dividing of time* (Daniel 7:25).

In the Book of Daniel chapter 7 we find this prophecy describing how the antichrist has taken control of the Earth. Daniel is referring to a fourth "beast" who will *"wear out the saints."* The method that he uses to "wear out" the saints is by changing times and laws. Daniel 7:25 literally says that the antichrist will afflict and torment God's people. He will change God's seasons and His decrees and laws, and God's people will yield to his power and authority. This should not be.

The word for *times* is *zemân*, which means season or time. The word for *laws* is the Hebrew word *dâth,* corresponding to decree, law.[1] I believe these two elements can be seen as the seasons of God and the Word of God.

In reference to the seasons of God, the devil is not necessarily trying to change the weather. This verse is referring to the seasonal festivals of God, also known as the Lord's feasts. God has His people observe certain feasts at specific times of the year. The fact that God is very specific as to when the festivals such as Passover, the Feast of Weeks, and the Feast of Tabernacles were to be observed gives us some indication of their importance.

God is so concerned with the feast days that most of the major events in Church history have happened during the celebration of the feasts. Jesus was crucified during Passover, and He ascended into Heaven during the Feast of Pentecost. He also established the first covenant during Pentecost. I believe the Scriptures are very clear that Jesus was born during the Feast of Tabernacles. Exodus 25:8 and John 1:14 talk about the time when God Himself came and dwelt (tabernacled) among His people.

We will discuss the feasts further in upcoming chapters, but I wanted to establish the point that God implemented a cycle or calendar that He would use to do big things. The devil is aware of this calendar, so he has sought to get the Church away from these cycles so that he can disconnect God's people from what God is trying to do amongst them.

The second device that the devil used to defeat the saints in Daniel 7 was to change the "laws" of God. I believe that this statement points to the fact that if the devil can take the Word of God away from the people, or even change and distort the Word, he can weaken the saints and, therefore, win the battle with them. When believers don't have the true Word of God, satan has been able to hinder part of the power source that we as believers have in our weapons arsenal.

In Section III, I will show how the enemy of God, the devil, has been working diligently to remove the truth of the Word of God from the saints. Our lack of knowledge, misunderstanding of warfare, and failure to fight our true enemy have caused us to become a weak shadow of the early Church of Jesus Christ.

GOD PROVIDES THE SOLUTION

I know that the Bible is a book of prophecy. Everything in the Bible has happened, is happening, or will happen. I hear many saints who take the attitude that since the Bible says something will happen, we should just sit by and let it take place. I disagree. The Scriptures tell us that when Jesus ascended into Heaven He told His followers that they were to wait in Jerusalem until the promised power, sent from the Father, would come. That power, the Holy Spirit, gives us supernatural abilities here on the Earth. Jesus also told Christians to *"occupy till I come"* (see Luke 19:13). This was in the context of a parable Jesus gave to demonstrate that we are given abilities and power and that they are to be used to increase the Kingdom for the Lord. As a matter of fact, the lord in the parable was very angry with the servants who did nothing with what they were given.

Whenever we see negative results in the Bible, it is a result of God's people not doing what they are supposed to do. In the Old Testament the Israelites were taken into captivity because they disobeyed God. When they obeyed God and followed His ways, they were able to defeat all their enemies, no matter how great. At the time that the Book of Daniel was written, the children of Israel were in captivity because they were not doing what God had required them to do. I see many

Christians living in defeat today, but I believe that once we reconnect with God, that can change.

In this same Book of Daniel, God provides us the solution to the problem of the saints of God losing the battle to the evil one here on the Earth. The beautiful thing about our God is that He is a problem-solver. Whenever God tells us about a problem, He then offers us the solution. God gives us the keys to solve every problem, and since the day of Pentecost, we have been empowered by the Holy Spirit to overcome every difficulty. The only reason that God even mentions these difficulties is to provide us with the solution. The only reason we were told that darkness was upon the face of the Earth was so that we could know the God who spoke light into existence. The only reason we were taught that humans are fallen and a sinful creature is so that He can teach us about redemption and salvation through Jesus Christ. What an awesome God we serve!

As we open our understanding to see how the enemy has weakened the Church through changing times and laws, we can learn to implement God's solutions to these problems. We can exchange defeat and captivity for victory!

Chapter 3

THE RELATIONSHIP BETWEEN GOD AND HUMANKIND

LET'S START FROM "THE BEGINNING"

*In the **beginning** God created the heaven and the earth* (Genesis 1:1).

God's purpose for creating the world and everything in it was to have a dwelling place to fellowship with the only being in the universe that was made in God's image—humankind. The word for "in the beginning" is *breshit,* which is most accurately translated as "for the sake of the beginning."[1] So the actual Hebrew translation of the first verse of the Bible is "for the sake of the beginning, God made the heavens and the earth." God's people, His Word, and the Messiah (Jesus) are all seen as "the beginning." Without going into a Hebrew lesson, this word shows us that we are the focus of God's attention and the sole purpose for the creation of the Earth.

We know that Jesus Christ is the Alpha and the Omega, the beginning and the end. Jesus is the intersection between God and humanity. Therefore, we see that the purpose for all creation is for God to have a place to commune with humankind, the only part of creation that is made in His image. We were not a side effect or an afterthought; we were the sole purpose of God creating the universe and all that is in it. That is why God takes our relationship with Him very seriously—to put it mildly. Seeing that we are the purpose for creation and not just a side effect should change how we view our relationship with God.

THE PURPOSE FOR HUMANITY

God's purpose for humankind is given in the Scripture known as the Adamic Covenant:

> *And God blessed them, and God said unto them, Be fruit-*
> *ful, and multiply, and replenish the earth, and subdue it: and*
> *have dominion over the fish of the sea, and over the fowl of the*
> *air, and over every living thing that moveth upon the earth*
> (Genesis 1:28).

God set up all things on Earth for humankind to have dominion, to rule in His image, and to commune with Him. He intended for humanity to live according to His design and to reap the benefits of doing so.

HUMANITY'S FALL FROM RELATIONSHIP

However, satan did not want to share Earth with humankind and sought to interfere in humanity's relationship with God.

> *And when the woman saw that the tree was good for food, and*
> *that it was pleasant to the eyes, and a tree to be desired to make*
> *one wise, she took of the fruit thereof, and did eat, and gave*
> *also unto her husband with her; and he did eat* (Genesis 3:6).

Here again we see the results of satan's subtle deception. He was able to deceive Eve by getting her to doubt God's Word and His intentions for humankind. If Eve had really believed that God's Word was true and that His plan for them was better than the alternate plan that the devil offered, she would have continued to follow God and rejected the alternate option.

After the Fall of Adam and Eve, God began a process of drawing humankind to reconnect with Him.

THE ABRAHAMIC COVENANT

God searched for someone to call apart to Himself and found Abram (later called Abraham).

> *Now the LORD had said unto Abram, Get thee out of thy country, and from thy kindred, and from thy father's house, unto a land that I will shew thee: And I will make of thee a great nation, and I will bless thee, and make thy name great; and thou shalt be a blessing: And I will bless them that bless thee, and curse him that curseth thee: and in thee shall all families of the earth be blessed* (Genesis 12:1-3).

> *And it came to pass, that, when the sun went down, and it was dark, behold a smoking furnace, and a burning lamp that passed between those pieces. In the same day the LORD made a covenant with Abram, saying, Unto thy seed have I given this land, from the river of Egypt unto the great river, the river Euphrates* (Genesis 15:17-18).

I'd like to interject something at this point: The Bible doesn't say it, but what if God had searched the entire world at that time and looked to find a person who would accept His offer of a covenant? Maybe God tried other people before Abram, but they failed the test. Maybe they were more interested in following the crowd, staying in the land they were familiar with, and were not willing to give up everything for God. Wouldn't that make Abram's willingness to completely surrender to God even more impressive? It's just something to think about.

With Abraham, God began to reinstate what was lost in the Garden of Eden. This was the first step back to God's original intention from the time of creation.

THE COVENANT WITH JACOB

The covenant with Jacob is something that really needs to be understood. First, as part of the promise that God made to Abraham, the blessed bloodline had to come down through Abraham's children. Isaac was the son that God had promised to give Abraham and Sarah; Jacob, being Isaac's son, was a suitable heir.

Through Jacob, God gave many prophetic messages. To go into great detail would take another book entirely, but I will briefly describe several:

1) Jacob wasn't the firstborn; Esau was. Since Esau was the oldest, he should have rightfully received the birthright and been the heir of Isaac. Because Esau took for granted the privilege of being the heir of his father, Jacob received the birthright instead. This is like what happened with Israel and the gentiles. Israel was supposed to be the rightful heir of God, but because they took it for granted, the gentiles now receive the blessing.

2) Jacob was born into the family of the covenant, but it wasn't until he wrestled with God that his name changed to Israel, and he then walked into the fullness of what God had waiting for him. Jacob went from the flesh to the faith; this is somewhat of a prophetic demonstration of the transition from the Old to the New Covenant. The Bible tells us that under the new covenant we are no longer in

covenant by the cutting of the flesh, but our circumcision happens in the hearts through faith in the Messiah, Jesus.

3)   As is described in the Book of Genesis, the covenant with Jacob is fulfilled because a "company of nations" would come out of his loins because of how much he valued the blessings promised to his fathers. The word for company of nations has the same meaning as the word for church in the New Testament. God was promising Jacob that the Church would come from his seed. This is important to bridge the gap between Israel and the New Testament Church. Because most New Testament churches have not properly recognized the connection between the two, ideas like replacement theology have been able to creep in. Replacement theology has convinced the New Testament Church that there is no real connection between the Old Testament and New Testament believers and, therefore, no necessity to understand the Old Testament types and shadows thoroughly.

> *And God said unto him, Thy name is Jacob: thy name shall not be called any more Jacob, but Israel shall be thy name: and He called his name Israel. And God said unto him, I am* **God Almighty**: *be fruitful and multiply; a nation and a company of nations shall be of thee, and kings shall come out of thy loins* (Genesis 35:10-11).

A side note: The name God Almighty is the Hebrew name *El Shaddai*. El Shaddai, the Almighty God, is one of the names that Isaiah 9:6 tells us the Messiah will be called. Therefore, it is Jesus, the *Logos,* who made the covenant with Jacob. When we worship the "Holy one of Israel" we are talking about the Messiah, Jesus. I mention this because when we understand the Holy Trinity, the original language of the Bible confirms the concept of the Trinity. The Bible makes a clear distinction regarding what person of the Godhead is speaking at different times. We worship one God who is complex in nature and who reveals

Himself in three unique characteristics. That is why Genesis refers to God as *Elohim,* which is a plural name for the Creator. Of course, we do not believe in three Gods, just One who has three separate but equal identities.

This means even more when we look at what happened on Calvary. Jesus made the covenant with humankind through Abraham, Isaac, and Jacob. It was also Jesus at Mount Sinai who gave the Law to Moses. Therefore, it had to be Jesus at Calvary who fulfilled the Law and who made a New Covenant with the seed of Abraham—the Church!

THE MOSAIC COVENANT

God gave His promise to the Israelites through Moses in Exodus 19:3-8:

> *And Moses went up unto God, and the LORD called unto him out of the mountain, saying, Thus shalt thou say to the **house of Jacob**, and tell the **children of Israel**; ye have seen what I did unto the Egyptians, and how I bare you on eagles' wings, and brought you unto Myself. Now therefore, if ye will obey My voice indeed, and keep My covenant, then ye shall be a peculiar treasure unto Me above all people: for all the earth is Mine: And ye shall be unto Me a kingdom of priests, and an holy nation. These are the words which thou shalt speak unto the children of Israel. And Moses came and called for the elders of the people, and laid before their faces all these words which the LORD commanded him. And all the people answered together, and said, All that the LORD hath spoken we will do. And Moses returned the words of the people unto the LORD.*

We see here that God spoke through Moses to two different groups of people: the house of Jacob (physical Jews) and the children of Israel (those who entered into covenant, but were not natural-born Jews). This second group comprised the "mixed multitude." This is the group that God declared to be His special people. The stipulation was that whoever entered into agreement with God's covenant would be considered His people. He used Abraham's seed to put this into effect, but only those agreeing with His Word could enter in.

THE MIXED MULTITUDE

And a mixed multitude went up also with them; and flocks, and herds, even very much cattle (Exodus 12:38).

From the very beginning, God always accepted those who had a desire to enter into covenant with Him. From the time He revealed His power to the pharaoh in Egypt, His call was for any person who would accept the terms of His covenant through obedience to it. Those who identified themselves as covenant people simply had to obey the God of Abraham, Isaac, and Jacob. They entered in by killing a lamb and smearing the blood over the doorpost of their dwelling. God gave His people a prophetic gesture in the natural world that would carry them over until the true Lamb of God, the Messiah, would rescue them once and for all from the eternal bondage of sin!

God always has used types and shadows to show us what will happen in the spirit realm. His prophetic gestures give us a deeper understanding of how He operates. A shadow shows an impression of the real event that is taking place. There has to be an original object in order for there to be a shadow. The other thing about a shadow is that we need light in order to see the shadow. God's Word is a light, and it allows us to see the actual spiritual events that the shadows represent.

God takes His people to a place where they must either accept or reject what He is doing. He wants to make things plain and simple.

This simplicity allows Him to righteously judge rebellion. When Jesus came to offer salvation to the nation of Israel, they knew exactly who He claimed to be; the only question was whether or not they would accept His claims.

As He always has, God puts the offer out to "whosoever" agrees with His Word. Agreement allows us to receive the blessings for which God has made provision. Obedience to the Word is where the blessings lie. In Exodus, it wasn't the identity of the people that caused them to be blessed; it was their agreement with His Word that created the covenant with God. The same is still true today.

REMINDER OF WHY THE COVENANT WAS MADE

For thou art an holy people unto the Lord thy God: the Lord thy God hath chosen thee to be a special people unto Himself, above all people that are upon the face of the earth. The Lord did not set His love upon you, nor choose you, because ye were more in number than any people; for ye were the fewest of all people: But because the Lord loved you, and because He would keep the oath which He had sworn unto your fathers, hath the Lord brought you out with a mighty hand, and redeemed you out of the house of bondmen, from the hand of Pharaoh king of Egypt (Deuteronomy 7:6-8).

Here God is letting His people know that they received the covenant not because they earned it, but because of the promise that He made to Abraham. God revealed that Israel was chosen and separated from the rest of the world simply because they were the descendants of Abraham. God searched for someone to make a covenant with and Abraham accepted the call. God set the terms of the agreement, and their ability to receive the benefits of the covenant came through agreeing with God's Word.

Replacement theology attempts to demonstrate how the New Testament Church has replaced the physical seed of Abraham, Isaac, and Jacob. I have heard it said that the Jews are no longer God's "chosen people." I do not share that belief. I believe it is clear that God will never break His covenant with Jacob.

As Bible-believing Christians, we must always acknowledge the Jews as our brothers and sisters whom we are to honor and love. We were adopted into the family of the Jews, not the other way around. As the Church, we must pray for the Jews to receive the Messiah. We must also honor them and have love for them because this is what brings God pleasure. The blessings and the love of the blood-bought believers in the Messiah are what should provoke the Jews to jealousy and ultimately win them for Jesus.

Chapter 4

WHAT IS THE NEW COVENANT?

THE PROMISE OF THE NEW COVENANT

God made the Mosaic Covenant with the Israelites, but He also gave the promise of another covenant, an everlasting one, that He would make with His people.

> *Moreover I will make a covenant of peace with them; it shall be an everlasting covenant with them: and I will place them, and multiply them, and will set My sanctuary in the midst of them for evermore. My tabernacle also shall be with them: yea, I will be their God, and they shall be My people. And the heathen shall know that I the* LORD *do sanctify Israel, when My sanctuary shall be **in the midst** of them for evermore* (Ezekiel 37:26-28).

> *Behold, the days come, saith the* LORD, *that I will make a new covenant with the house of Israel, and with the house of Judah: Not according to the covenant that I made with their fathers in the day that I took them by the hand to bring them out of the land of Egypt; which My covenant they brake, although I was an husband unto them, saith the* LORD: *But this shall be the*

*covenant that I will make with the house of Israel; After those
days, saith the LORD, I will put My law in their inward parts,
and write it in their hearts; and will be their God, and they
shall be My people* (Jeremiah 31:31-33).

When this verse says *"My law,"* it is referring to the Torah, which is
the written law that we know as the first five books of the Bible (we will
look at this is greater detail in Section IV). The Lord (Jesus) is saying
that in the New Covenant, the Law will be written on believers' hearts
instead of on tablets of stone.

These are very important Scriptures because this is how God said
He would transition from the Old Covenant to the New. Notice that
when He speaks through His servants the prophets, He is telling His
people that a new agreement is coming.

God prophetically spoke that when the New Covenant was made,
God Himself would dwell inside of His people, *"in the midst of them."*
He says through the prophet Jeremiah that the Law that defined the
old agreement between Him and His people would now be written on
their hearts. He never said that the Law of the covenant itself would be
changed, just the way it is enacted. Instead of a physical temple where
actual animals were killed, His people would become the temple. Instead
of the Law written on tablets and parchments, it would be written on
their hearts. And instead of cutting the flesh through outward circumcision, the piercing would happen on the inside.

WHO BROKE THE COVENANT?

The people who received Moses' Law had stony hearts; they would
not receive it by faith. God said that He was a husband to them even
while they broke His covenant. The Book of Hebrews reiterates this
idea of God *"finding fault with them"*:

But now hath He obtained a more excellent ministry, by how much also He is the mediator of a better covenant, which was established upon better promises. For if that first covenant had been faultless, then should no place have been sought for the second. **For finding fault with them,** *He saith, Behold, the days come, saith the Lord, when* **I will make a new covenant** *with the house of Israel and with the house of Judah: Not according to the covenant that I made with their fathers in the day when I took them by the hand to lead them out of the land of Egypt; because they continued not in My covenant, and I regarded them not, saith the Lord. For this is the covenant that* **I will make with the house of Israel after those days, saith the Lord; I will put My laws into their mind, and write them in their hearts:** *and I will be to them a God, and they shall be to Me a people* (Hebrews 8:6-10).

The Word of God is perfect; it was the people who received the covenant who had the problem. Since the children of Israel could not keep the old covenant, God made a new one and gave them some added power to assist them.

The Bible tells us that Jesus was slain before the foundation of the world (see Rev. 13:8). We also know that God knew the plan for salvation even before Jesus was born. These facts confirm that God did not give the first covenant and then become surprised that men and women could not keep it. That is the reason for God's grace. God set a standard; He actually is the only perfect One who is able to meet the standard. Because God knew this, He made provision for redemption through the Messiah. We can never believe that there was something wrong with God's portion of the covenant. Since He knows all, He doesn't have a reason to change His mind regarding His feelings toward humankind.

Again, the Bible says that the people who were given the covenant failed; God did not.

Through the new birth and the Holy Spirit, God gives us a heart of flesh in which the Holy Spirit convicts us of sin (see John 16). The Holy Spirit also helps us to overcome our old sin nature, thereby strengthening our ability to keep God's Word.

JESUS EXPLAINS THE NEW COVENANT

And as they were eating, Jesus took bread, and blessed it, and brake it, and gave it to the disciples, and said, Take, eat; this is My body. And He took the cup, and gave thanks, and gave it to them, saying, Drink ye all of it; for this is My blood of the new testament, which is shed for many for the remission of sins. But I say unto you, I will not drink henceforth of this fruit of the vine, until that day when I drink it new with you in My Father's kingdom (Matthew 26:26-29).

Likewise also the cup after supper, saying, This cup is the new testament in My blood, which is shed for you (Luke 22:20).

As Jesus reminded His disciples of the promise of the New Covenant, He informed them that His body and blood would take the place of the animals previously required by the Father. He also let them know that the offer was not focused on the physical seed of Abraham, but the focus is on the entire world. Remember, He told Abraham that all the nations would be blessed because of his obedience.

And other sheep I have, which are not of this fold: them also I must bring, and they shall hear My voice; and there shall be one fold, and one shepherd (John 10:16).

Jesus mentions the sheep that He has from another fold. Who are these sheep? Jesus' primary ministry was geared toward the seed of Abraham. To fulfill the promise made in Genesis, He first offered the New Covenant to the Jews, and after they did not receive it as a nation, God then turned the offer to all other nations.

God Begins Replenishing His Church

Therefore let all the house of Israel know assuredly, that God hath made the same Jesus, whom ye have crucified, both Lord and Christ. Now when they heard this, they were pricked in their heart, and said unto Peter and to the rest of the apostles, Men and brethren, what shall we do? Then Peter said unto them, Repent, and be baptized every one of you in the name of Jesus Christ for the remission of sins, and ye shall receive the gift of the Holy Ghost. For the promise is unto you, and to your children, and to all that are afar off, even as many as the LORD our God shall call. And with many other words did he testify and exhort, saying, Save yourselves from this untoward generation. Then they that gladly received his word were baptized: and the same day there were added unto them about **three thousand souls** *(Acts 2:36-41).*

In Acts 2:41, 3,000 souls were added to the Church. This was to replace the 3,000 lost in the wilderness:

And the children of Levi did according to the word of Moses: and there fell of the people that day about three thousand men (Exodus 32:28).

Soon after God made the covenant with Israel in the wilderness, the people demonstrated the hardness of their hearts by violating the Law. To show them what sin does to people spiritually, God had the violators killed. Like Adam and Eve, when they broke God's Law, it brought forth death. The Bible tells us that the wages of sin is death (see Rom. 6:23).

Since God is the source of life, to turn away from God brings death. Under the Old Covenant, many times God had this literally acted out: When people broke the commandments, they were put to death. Because God operates in types and shadows, He showed them in the natural world what was happening to them spiritually.

Of course, we know that Jesus came to bring us closer to God. He literally came to bring us back to life by reconnecting us to life Himself. The Creator, who is the source of life, gave us life by redeeming us back to Himself. He demonstrated that by adding 3,000 souls to replace the 3,000 lost under the Old Covenant.

In the next chapter we will further examine the connection between God's people under the Old Covenant and His New Covenant people.

Chapter 5

WHO IS THE CHURCH?

ONE CHURCH, TWO COVENANTS

The actual language of the Bible does not differentiate between the people who make up the Church in the Old Testament and in the New Testament. Throughout the Bible, the words *assembly, synagogue,* and *church* all have the same meaning, whether from the Hebrew word *kahal* or the Greek word *ecclesia.* They all represent a group of people who are called out to be holy and separated for God's purpose. Under the Old Covenant, they were separated through circumcision and the temple rights, and in the New Covenant they are separated by faith in the Messiah, Jesus.

> *This is he* [Moses], *that was in **the church in the wilderness** with the angel which spake to him in the mount Sina, and with our fathers: who received the lively oracles to give unto us* (Acts 7:38).

> *For if there come unto your **assembly** a man with a gold ring, in goodly apparel, and there come in also a poor man in vile raiment* (James 2:2).

*Behold, I will make them of the **synagogue** of Satan, which
say they are Jews, and are not, but do lie; behold, I will make
them to come and worship before thy feet, and to know that I
have loved thee* (Revelation 3:9).

There is no difference between these words *church, synagogue,* and
assembly. They simply mean a "called out assembly." The Hebrew word
in the Old Testament, *kahal,* is cross referenced to the Greek word *ecclesia* in the New Testament.[1] God never specified a difference in the terms.

People have attempted to make a difference between these two
groups of people and separate the Church of the Old Testament from
the Church of the New Testament. This is mainly because of a lack
of understanding of the continuation of God's relationship between
humankind and Himself. Many of the early Church fathers also gar-
nered a very strong anti-Semitic tone. They wanted to draw a large gap
between the Church and Israel and between the New Testament and the
Old. The only differentiation that God made was that under the Old
Testament the people had a written Law to follow and under the New
Testament the Holy Spirit writes God's Law on the hearts of His people.

JACOB BECOMES ISRAEL

*And God said unto him, Thy name is Jacob: thy name shall
not be called any more Jacob, but Israel shall be thy name: and
He called his name Israel. And God said unto him, I am God
Almighty: be fruitful and multiply; **a nation and a company
of nations** shall be of thee, and kings shall come out of thy
loins* (Genesis 35:10-11).

The word for a "company of nations" here is a *kahal!* When Jacob
went from flesh to faith, God promised that out of his loins would
come a *"called out assembly."* God was telling Jacob that the Church

would come from his seed. The promise to Abraham was that *"all the nations of the world"* would be blessed through his seed (see Gen. 12:3). God kept that promise to Abraham because the Messiah and salvation were passed down through the physical Jews.

The word *nations* here is important; it helps to reinforce the fact that, although the promise was made through Abraham, God always had the entire world in mind, not just the Jews. The Jews have not been forsaken, but they are just a part of the larger plan of God to get the rest of the world saved.

> *And Moses went up unto God, and the LORD called unto him out of the mountain, saying, Thus shalt thou say to the house of Jacob, and tell the children of Israel* (Exodus 19:3).

As we saw in the previous chapter, two groups of people came out of Egypt when God delivered the Israelites from bondage: *"the house of Jacob,"* the physical Jews, and *"the children of Israel,"* the people of faith (the mixed multitude, non-Jews).

> *Now therefore, **if ye will obey My voice indeed, and keep My covenant, then ye shall be a peculiar treasure unto Me above all people**: for all the earth is Mine: And ye shall be unto Me a kingdom of priests, and an holy nation. These are the words which thou shalt speak unto **the children of Israel**. And Moses came and called for the elders of the people, and laid before their faces all these words which the LORD commanded him. And all the people answered together, and said, All that the LORD hath spoken we will do. And Moses returned the words of the people unto the LORD* (Exodus 19:5-8).

Only those people who agreed to the terms of the covenant were considered God's people. At that time, the outward sign that they were in agreement was the circumcision. One of the major commandments of the Old Covenant was that the fathers had to diligently teach their children the laws of the covenant. The outward sign of obeying the covenant was the requirement to circumcise all males. The father was considered the priest of the household, and the teaching of the Law was to be carried on through the passing down of the priesthood by the males.

In Exodus 12, God told His people that if they kept the covenant (the Law), then they were His people. He even said that those who were Gentiles in the flesh who willingly entered into covenant with God were just like those who were born Jews.

> *And when a stranger shall sojourn with thee, and will keep the passover to the LORD, let all his males be circumcised, and then let him come near and keep it; and he shall be as one that is born in the land: for no uncircumcised person shall eat thereof. One law shall be to him that is homeborn, and unto the stranger that sojourneth among you* (Exodus 12:48-49).

The circumcision was a sign in the flesh that they were entering into covenant with God. Once they accepted the terms of the covenant, even those who were not born Jews became God's people. God confirmed to them that they were made Covenant people because of the promise to Abraham:

> *The LORD did not set his love upon you, nor choose you, because ye were more in number than any people; for ye were the fewest of all people: But **because the LORD loved you, and because he would keep the oath which he had sworn unto your fathers,** hath the LORD brought you out with a mighty hand, and redeemed you out of the house of bondmen, from the hand of Pharaoh king of Egypt* (Deuteronomy 7:7-8)

When the people broke the Law, they were out of covenant with God. That is why the 3,000 people who broke the first commandment and worshiped another God were all killed by Aaron and the priests. They had broken the covenant and were put to death.

The covenants were always about keeping God's Word. A covenant was never about the people who kept it. The only person in this deal who had an unconditional agreement with God was Abraham, and that was because he passed God's test of total obedience. God was looking for a people to make a covenant with, and He saw that Abraham would value the covenant more than anything in the world.

> *And said, By Myself have I sworn, saith the LORD, for because thou hast done this thing, and hast not withheld thy son, thine only son: That in blessing I will bless thee, and in multiplying I will multiply thy seed as the stars of the heaven, and as the sand which is upon the sea shore; and thy seed shall possess the gate of his enemies; And in thy seed shall all the nations of the earth be blessed; because thou hast obeyed My voice* (Genesis 22:16-18).

THE FAMILY CONNECTION BETWEEN THE CHURCH AND ISRAEL

> *For ye are all the children of God by faith in Christ Jesus. For as many of you as have been baptized into Christ have put on Christ. There is neither Jew nor Greek, there is neither bond nor free, there is neither male nor female: for ye are all one in Christ Jesus. And if ye be Christ's, then are ye Abraham's seed, and heirs according to the promise* (Galatians 3:26-29).

Once we are saved, we become Abraham's seed and are heirs according to the covenant made with Abraham!

Paul reconfirms the fact that under the New Covenant, through faith in the Messiah, we become a family along with the physical Jews and receive the blessing of the covenant that was given to Abraham. Through faith in Jesus, there is no difference between Jew and Gentile. The blessing is based on faith, and that faith is demonstrated by receiving the sacrifice of the Lamb of God, Jesus Christ! Instead of circumcision and animal sacrifices, we now simply confess with our mouths and believe in our hearts that we are saved by our resurrected Savior whose blood is spread across the mercy seat of the Holy of Holies in Heaven (see Heb. 9:11-24).

Romans 11:17 says that we have been grafted into the family of God through faith:

> *And if some of the branches be broken off, and thou, being a wild olive tree, wert **grafted in** among them, and with them partakest of the root and fatness of the olive tree.*

The words *grafted in* come from the Greek word *egkentrizō* (pronounced *eng-ken-trid'-zo) meaning* to "prick in," that is, "ingraft:—graff in (-to)."[2] The English definition of *graft* from the *Merriam-Webster Dictionary* is: "to unite, to join, to implant living tissue surgically."

The apostle Paul is telling us is that there is a family and then another family is grafted in and becomes a part of the original family. Think about a skin graft. If you grafted skin from your leg onto your arm, then the new skin would become a part of your arm.

Ephesians 1:5 says that God has *"...predestinated us unto the adoption of children by Jesus Christ to Himself, according to the good pleasure of His will."* Again, when we use this example, we see that if a person is adopted into the Jones family then they would become a Jones; they would become as much a part of the family as those born into the family.

This is what Paul is saying to the church in Ephesus—that God had pre-ordained that there would be an adoption of people into the family of God. The people of Ephesus were not necessarily "physical Jews," but because of their faith, they became a part of the family of God. They became one with the seed of Abraham.

THE MIDDLE WALL OF SEPARATION
HAS BEEN TORN DOWN

For He is our peace, who hath made both one, and hath broken down the middle wall of partition between us (Ephesians 2:14).

This speaks of the temple in which the Jews worshiped God. Only the priest was allowed to go into the Holy of Holies, and he had to go through a very intense sanctification process. If a priest was not correctly sanctified when he entered into the presence of God, he would die. His fellow priests even had to tie a rope around his ankle with a bell attached. If the priest was found not to be properly sanctified and died, no one else would have been able to go in and get him out. The rope was a means of pulling the priest out. (See Exodus 28:33-35.)

The other section of the temple was reserved for the Jews who were under the covenant. They could enter into the temple, but not into the Holy of Holies. There was also a wall in the temple that separated the covenant Jews from the Gentiles. The Gentiles were forbidden from entering past this wall.

The beautiful thing about our Messiah is that He broke down the wall of separation and tore the veil. So through faith in Jesus, we come all the way from outside the wall, and now we can come directly into the Most Holy Place. Our God is so good!

We are "one new man" in Christ Jesus!

Wherefore remember, that ye being in time past Gentiles in the flesh, who are called Uncircumcision by that which is called the Circumcision in the flesh made by hands; that at that time ye were without Christ, being aliens from the commonwealth *of Israel, and strangers from the covenants of promise, having no hope, and without God in the world: But now in Christ Jesus ye who sometimes were far off are made nigh by the blood of Christ. For He is our peace, who hath made both one, and hath broken down the middle wall of partition between us; having abolished in His flesh the enmity, even the law of commandments contained in ordinances; for to make in Himself of twain **one new man,** so making peace* (Ephesians 2:11-15).

Section II

CHANGING TIMES

"...and think to change times..."

Chapter 6

UNDERSTANDING GOD'S "APPOINTED TIMES"

Remember what Daniel 7:25 says:

> *And he shall speak great words against the most High, and shall wear out the saints of the most High,* **and think to change times** *[seasons] and laws [the Word of God]....*

As we have said, the word *times* is from the Chaldean word *zemân* (pronounced *zem-awn'*), meaning "season or time."[1] This particular set of Scriptures was written originally in Chaldean because this was the language adopted by Israel while they were living in captivity in Babylon. So, one of the devices the enemy has used to weaken the Body of Christ is by changing our understanding of time. The antichrist will wear out (torment and afflict) God's people by changing the seasons of God.

The upcoming chapters will look at when the devil changed the seasons of God. But first, let's look at these appointed times.

GOD'S CALENDAR VS. HUMANITY'S CALENDAR

Many Scriptures in the Old Testament are devoted to describing the calendar that God set for His people to follow. This calendar revolves around a cycle of annual festivals. I believe that satan's plan is to get

God's people out of sync with the cycle that God has given us that allows us to be in sync with each other and in sync with God. It is difficult for us to get a deeper understanding of God when we are "out of sync" with the seasons of God. As long as satan can keep us off balance and out of touch with God, then he is able to wear us out and to overcome the saints. I believe that God is giving us new revelation about God's cycles in order to get us in a position of power to reclaim much of the territory that we have lost.

WHAT ARE THE SEASONS OF GOD?

And the LORD spake unto Moses, saying, Speak unto the children of Israel, and say unto them, Concerning the feasts of the LORD, which ye shall proclaim to be holy convocations, even these are my feasts. Six days shall work be done: but the seventh day is the sabbath of rest, an holy convocation; ye shall do no work therein: it is the sabbath of the LORD in all your dwellings. These are the feasts of the LORD, even holy convocations, which ye shall proclaim in their **seasons** *(Leviticus 23:1-4).*

In this Scripture in Leviticus, the word *seasons* comes from the Hebrew word *mô'êd*. *Strong's Concordance* defines this word as: "properly an appointment, that is, a fixed time or season; appointed (sign, time), (place of, solemn) assembly, congregation, (set, solemn) feast, (set) time (appointed)."[2]

Again we see here that God has certain "seasons" that He expects us to follow. We see without a shadow of a doubt that God is a God of purpose. Everything that God gives us to follow is for a reason. We will see that God didn't give us a list of observances "just because." We gain something of great importance from our obedience to do what God tells us to do. We also gain a deeper understanding when we observe the "appointed times" of God. *The seasons of God are God's appointed times that He has set and that He expects us to keep. He literally is saying that He will meet us during these times in a very special way.*

Of course the enemy understands the importance of these times. That is why he has been very strategic in his attempt to remove the feast days from our relationship with God. As long as he convinces us that they are no longer of any importance and we forsake them, then we lose. As was stated in Daniel 7:25, the antichrist overcomes the saints of God, and they are overpowered by him because he is able to change the seasons and the laws of God. If the enemy causes us to forsake these things, then we place ourselves into bondage. More importantly, we miss out on the abundant blessings and peace that come from being in unity with God.

COMING INTO AGREEMENT WITH GOD

I do not share about the feasts or the laws of God to bring condemnation to the Body of Christ; nor am I trying to lay a heavy burden on people. As we will see later on, when we forsake the laws of God, we enter into bondage, not the other way around. God's laws bring us liberty and freedom; we are blessed when we come into agreement with God and His Word. I teach on the way of the Lord because I know that the closer we follow God, the more we walk into victory and power. The further away we are from God through His Word, the more powerless we become and the more we walk in defeat. I believe that God is trying to reveal these things to us in this season because the time is short and the battle is about to intensify!

The Bible tells us that in order for two people to walk together, they must agree (see Amos 3:3). We need to understand that the way for us to agree with God is through our obedience to His Word. We don't bring anything to the table. We can only walk with God when we acknowledge that He is right and we are wrong. The Bible tells us that He wants obedience over sacrifice, meaning that we walk in the fullness of God by submitting our wills to the will of God.

God tells us that as far as the heavens are from the Earth, so far are His ways higher than ours (see Isa. 55:9). God wants us to know that we are not equals to Him. The way that we come into agreement is to simply acknowledge God and His Word and decide to follow Him. As God has demonstrated over and over again, once we obey Him and His Word, He reveals Himself to us in a much deeper way.

Obedience is not always easy, but it is simple. The more we obey the Word of God, the closer we draw to Him, and the more we can walk in the fullness of our relationship with God. We cannot always even understand why God tells us what He does. That is why it requires faith: faith that His Word is true, faith that He knows more than we do, and faith that following God's path brings us the power to walk as Christ did—the power that much of the Church is missing!

> *Whosoever therefore shall break one of these least command-ments, and shall teach men so, he shall be called the least in the kingdom of heaven: but whosoever shall do and teach them, the same shall be called great in the kingdom of heaven* (Matthew 5:19).

Chapter 7

THE FEASTS IN THE EARLY CHURCH

JESUS KEPT THE FEASTS

And it was at Jerusalem the feast of the dedication, and it was winter. And Jesus walked in the temple in Solomon's porch (John 10:22-23).

And the Jews' Passover was at hand, and Jesus went up to Jerusalem (John 2:13).

In the last day, that great day of the feast, Jesus stood and cried, saying, If any man thirst, let him come unto Me, and drink (John 7:37).

Then came the day of unleavened bread, when the passover must be killed. And He sent Peter and John, saying, Go and prepare us the passover, that we may eat (Luke 22:7-8).

And when the hour was come, He sat down, and the twelve apostles with Him. And He said unto them, With desire I have desired to eat this passover with you before I suffer: For I say unto you, I will not any more eat thereof, until it be fulfilled in the kingdom of God. And He took the cup, and gave

*thanks, and said, Take this, and divide it among yourselves:
For I say unto you, I will not drink of the fruit of the vine,
until the kingdom of God shall come. And He took bread,
and gave thanks, and brake it, and gave unto them, saying,
This is My body which is given for you: this do in remembrance of Me. Likewise also the cup after supper, saying, This
cup is the new testament in My blood, which is shed for you*
(Luke 22:14-20).

*For I have received of the Lord that which also I delivered
unto you, that the Lord Jesus the same night in which He
was betrayed took bread: And when He had given thanks,
He brake it, and said, Take, eat: this is My body, which is
broken for you: this do in remembrance of Me. After the same
manner also He took the cup, when He had supped, saying,
this cup is the new testament in My blood: this do ye, as oft as
ye drink it, in remembrance of Me. For as often as ye eat this
bread, and drink this cup, ye do shew the Lord's death till He
come* (1 Corinthians 11:23-26).

The first Church continued to celebrate the feasts of God for over
300 years.

Paul Continued to Keep the Law

The apostle Paul bragged about being a Pharisee 20 years after his
conversion

*But when Paul perceived that the one part were Sadducees,
and the other Pharisees, he cried out in the council, Men
and brethren, **I am a Pharisee**, the son of a Pharisee: of the
hope and resurrection of the dead I am called in question*
(Acts 23:6).

When Paul was being detained and went before the Sanhedrin, they could not put him to death because he had not broken the Law. The only things that he had to prove during his various incarcerations were: 1) he was not inciting riots to cause disruptions, and 2) he was not blaspheming by claiming that Jesus was the Son of God. Under Jewish Law, if a man who had taken the oath of a Pharisee was found to violate the Law, the council could have publicly put him to death. Therefore, at the time Paul went before the council, more than 20 years after being saved, he still kept the Law. This was the same Law in which the Jews found the perceived right to crucify Jesus for blasphemy because He claimed to be the Son of God. Keeping the Law included celebrating the feasts ordained by the Lord.

PAUL CONTINUED TO KEEP
THE LORD'S FEAST DAYS

We also know that Paul continued to celebrate the feasts after his conversion because he specifically says so:

> But bade them farewell, saying, **I must by all means keep this feast** that cometh in Jerusalem: but I will return again unto you, if God will. And he sailed from Ephesus (Acts 18:21).

> Purge out therefore the old leaven, that ye may be a new lump, as ye are unleavened. For even Christ our Passover is sacrificed for us: **Therefore let us keep the feast**, not with old leaven, neither with the leaven of malice and wickedness; but with the unleavened bread of sincerity and truth (1 Corinthians 5:7-8).

Paul obviously believed that the Lord's feast days and Sabbaths were meaningful; why else would he have continued to follow them?

PAUL REBUKED THE EARLY CONVERTS FOR
GOING BACK TO PAGAN OBSERVANCES

Paul not only kept the feasts himself, but he also addressed the matter in some of his letters to the new churches that were growing (see Gal. 4; 1 Cor. 10; Col. 2). The interesting thing about these Scriptures is that for many years we have misinterpreted them. I have heard them interpreted as Paul rebuking the early Church followers for going back to following the Law of Moses. When looking at these Scriptures more closely, we will see that Paul is not referring to the Law of Moses.

Think about the people he is writing to. The churches in the regions of Galatia, Corinth, and Colossae were in pagan regions. These regions had traditionally worshiped many false gods. Paul was encouraging these believers not to go back to their old pagan observances. They had not been observing the Lord's feast days or the Sabbaths. They were still following their own set of pagan holy days that had nothing to do with the biblical teachings.

> *Let no man therefore judge you in meat, or in drink, or in respect of an holyday, or of the new moon, or of the sabbath days: which are a **shadow** of things to come; but the body is of Christ* (Colossians 2:16-17).

Paul is telling the Colossians that they were not to let the people of their community judge them because of their new faith. They were formerly pagan, but now they are followers of the Word of God. As we know from the Scriptures, the feast days are simply shadows that point to Jesus as the Messiah.

> *Howbeit then, when ye knew not God, ye did service unto them which by nature are no gods. But now, after that ye have known God, or rather are known of God, how turn ye*

again to the weak and beggarly elements, whereunto ye desire
again to be in bondage? **Ye observe days, and months, and**
times, and years. I am afraid of you, lest I have bestowed
upon you labour in vain (Galatians 4:8-11).

Here again, Paul is not talking about the Lord's feast days; he is
telling the followers of Christ in Galatia not to go back to the pagan
observances that they once followed. The pagans worshiped many different gods, including the earth and the elements. They even worshiped
trees that they cut down and decorated (sound familiar?). The problem
was that the larger culture in the regions where they lived continued to
follow their pagan practices. Paul was getting frustrated with the believers so he reminded them that since they were now followers of Jesus
and not pagans, he expected them to stop their old ways and begin to
observe the Lord's feast days.

THE WORLD'S WAY OR GOD'S WAY

This has always been an issue: God's system versus the world's system.
God has always given His people a choice to choose either His way or
the way of the world. There has always been a conflict between the two.
That is why we are called "holy," "separated," and "set apart." The Bible
even calls us "peculiar" people. We were never meant to fit in; we are
called to be a group of people that operates under our own authority.

Now therefore, if ye will obey My voice indeed, and keep My
covenant, then ye shall be a peculiar treasure unto Me above all
people: for all the earth is Mine (Exodus 19:5).

Because it is written, Be ye holy; for I am holy (1 Peter 1:16).

For I am the LORD your God: ye shall therefore sanctify your-
selves, and ye shall be holy; for I am holy: neither shall ye defile

yourselves with any manner of creeping thing that creepeth upon the earth. For I am the LORD that bringeth you up out of the land of Egypt, to be your God: ye shall therefore be holy, for I am holy (Leviticus 11:44-45).

Since the Garden of Eden, there have been two competing systems: the system of the world, which is run by satan, and the Kingdom of God, which has its own cycle. The cycle of God brings life, peace, and blessings. Satan's cycle brings death and destruction. His system opposes God's system, and satan uses whatever means to get us on his cycle. He can use subtle means or obvious means. When we are not aware of his devices, we fall victim to his plan to get us on his cycle of death and destruction.

Chapter 8

ANTI-SEMITISM AND LEGALISM
IN THE EARLY CHURCH

ANTI-SEMITISM INVADES THE CHURCH

The greatest thing that satan has been able to do is to separate the Church from its foundation—not its Jewish roots, but its biblical roots! As we will see, the observances found in Leviticus 23 were designated by God. The Jews were simply following them because they were required by God to follow them. When they allowed the influences of the pagan nations to infiltrate their religious observances, they entered into judgment. They went into captivity and exile because they turned away from the commandments of God and began following the practices of the world. When they were aligned with the commandments of the Lord, they were a powerful nation. It is when satan is able to separate us from our power supply that we become truly powerless!

Satan was able to separate the Church from the direction God had put it on by convincing the Church fathers that the Lord's feasts were only for the Jews and that the Jews were enemies to God. Of course, that was never the case at all.

Several Church councils in the new "Christianity" from A.D. 341 to A.D. 626 prohibited Christians from celebrating the Sabbath and

"Jewish" festivals and even from eating with Jews. It seemed that the greatest concern with Judaism on the part of Christian leaders was the attraction that it held for Christians. These rules do not come out of bad relations between Jews and Christians (what would now be called, erroneously, anti-Semitism), but rather they were enacted because relations were good and the authorities wanted to separate the two peoples. God has always had a remnant that has followed the Torah. Obviously, if the Christians were not following the feast days and Sabbaths for the first 300 years of the Church, then there would have been no reason to pass declarations forbidding them to do so.

Legalism

Origen, A.D.185-254, was the Church leader most responsible for changing the way the Church interpreted prophecy, which created an atmosphere in which Christian anti-Semitism took root and spread. He developed a new teaching on "legalism," setting the stage throughout history for the term "legalism" becoming synonymous with Judaism and for both being condemned.

Origen also played a huge role in the misinterpretation of biblical doctrine, which caused the changing of the translations of the original Scriptures. These false teachings, along with the anti-Semitic beliefs introduced into Christianity, have had a very damaging effect on the Church. Many of these negative effects are still being felt many centuries later.

Webster's Dictionary defines *legalism* as "the doctrine of salvation by good works."

The term *legalism* has been misused by many people to indicate the teaching of following the laws of God. Some present-day teachings say that following the Old Testament is legalistic. *Legalism is not teaching followers to follow the Torah!* The Bible clearly states that following the Torah brings liberty while turning away from the Law of God brings bondage. We will discuss this in more depth in Section IV.

The Bible teaches that blessings and liberty come from following Torah (God's laws). Once we grasp this concept, then we are able to see how strategic the enemy has been in getting God's people away from the foundational teachings of the Old Covenant, but more specifically the Torah. The devil wants us to be in bondage, even if it is a religious bondage. Religious bondage pulls us away from God just like anything else. The devil knows that as long as he can separate us from God, then he has the power to overcome us. God is our power source, and the closer we get to God, the more empowered we are to destroy the works of the devil!

Blessing

Rather than being legalistic or bringing bondage, the Law of God brings blessing. *The Merriam Webster Dictionary* defines the word *blessing* as: "The act of invoking divine protection or aid; approval; good wishes; the bestowal of a divine gift or favour."

While there is no Greek word for *blessed,* the closest meaning in Greek is the word *eulogeitos,* which is where we get the word *eulogy,* meaning "to speak well of." The Hebrew word for *blessed* comes from the word *baruch* or *barak*: to kneel, bless, praise. The word appears both as a verb and as a noun. From the root *barakh* are derived other words, such as *barukh* (blessed), *berekh* (knee), and *b'rakha* (blessing), thus implying an association between humbling ourselves (i.e., kneeling before the Lord in submission and obedience) and receiving personal blessing from Him.[1]

Through our obedience to God's Word and His ways, we receive His favor, approval, and the bestowal of divine gifts.

WHAT THE BIBLE SAYS ABOUT FOLLOWING GOD'S LAW

Blessed is the man that walketh not in the counsel of the ungodly, nor standeth in the way of sinners, nor sitteth in

*the seat of the scornful. But his delight is in the law of the
LORD; and in His law doth he meditate day and night*
(Psalm 1:1-2).

We are blessed when we follow the Law and meditate on it day
and night.

*So shall I keep thy law continually for ever and ever. And I
will walk at liberty: for I seek Thy precepts* (Psalm 119:44-45).

We walk in liberty when we keep the law.

Later in the book, we will see that God wants to bring us back to the
teaching of the Law of Moses. It is the teaching of the Law that brings
us peace, blessings, and power. When we observe the Lord's feast days,
we come into agreement with God, which empowers us like nothing
else. Just think about this: If there was nothing special about the feast
days, then why did God devote so much Scripture to them? Why was
the Messiah's life so closely connected with the feasts? And why was so
much hatred and animosity focused on those who were observing the
feasts of the Lord?

The Ministry of Elijah Returns the Children to the Fathers

*Remember ye the Law of Moses My servant, which I com-
manded unto him in Horeb for all Israel, with the statutes and
judgments. Behold, I will send you Elijah the prophet before
the coming of the great and dreadful day of the LORD: And he
shall turn the heart of the fathers to the children, and the heart
of the children to their fathers, lest I come and smite the earth
with a curse* (Malachi 4:4-6).

*Fathers= (Strong's H1), forefathers (i.e. Abraham, Isaac, and
Jacob, emphasis mine)*

This passage in Malachi is not simply referring to turning biological sons back to their biological fathers. The word for fathers is making a reference to spiritual fathers. Abraham, Isaac, and Jacob are considered the "spiritual fathers" of all who have faith in God. It also tells us to remember the Law of Moses. This connects the New Testament believers to those whom God used as a foundation of the family of God. The Spirit of God will connect the Church to Israel before the Lord Jesus returns.

The major problem occurred when a strong spirit of anti-Semitism gained a foothold in the Church. It started very early on and grew stronger with time. We will now see how satan used this spirit to change times.

Chapter 9

THE INFLUENCE OF CONSTANTINE

Origen wasn't the only Church father who introduced harmful concepts into the Church. Another major figure in early Christianity, the Roman emperor Constantine, also had a major impact. Constantine is well known for taking Christianity from the status of being an outlawed religion in the Roman Empire to being the official Roman religion. But in the process of making Church practices more acceptable in Rome, he separated them from their foundations and introduced paganism into the Church. He did like many before him have done, which is to mix religious practices of the true worship of God and the false god worship, something that the Lord repeatedly forbids.

What did he change?

Mithra and Tammuz

While Emperor Constantine was praying to the Roman sun god, Mithra, he received "divine" instructions for a renewed and improved religion to unify the Roman Empire. Constantine declared Christianity to be the state religion and consecrated himself as "Pontifex Maximus," a title reserved for the high priest of paganism. He united his subjects under the sign of "the cross of Mithra," which had already decorated the Roman battle standards for over a hundred years. It happened to be the same symbol that the Persians borrowed from the Babylonian worshipers of the "god" Tammuz.

Constantine invented "another Jesus" (see 2 Cor. 11:4) to replace Tammuz and adorned him with all the accoutrements of Mithra worship.

CONSTANTINE'S JESUS

The Mixture of the "Son" God and the "Sun" God

Notice the circle around Jesus' head. This is how the new religion created by Emperor Constantine defined Jesus. He is a mixture of the God of Christianity and the gods of paganism. The Roman goddess "Easter" was also deposed and replaced by the "Virgin Mary" as the new "queen of heaven."

Constantine also mixed religions by taking the pagan holy days and branding them with Christian meanings.

The Roman Calendar

The "sun calendar," also known as the Julian calendar, was the official calendar of the Roman Empire, and it is still used in many places that were influenced by ancient Rome. Long before the time of Constantine, the Babylonian priests of Nimrod had already divided the year into the four quarters of the solar cycle: the winter and summer solstices and the vernal and autumnal equinoxes.

The Romans then haphazardly parceled 28 to 31 day months around the solar year, and named the months to honor their fictitious gods. The year begins with January, named for Janus, the two-headed god who looks back at the past and forward to the future. The span of February through June is populated with the personalities of various fallen angels. Julius and Augustus, emperors who were believed to have become gods, are honored by the midsummer months. September through December are the only months that remain numbered and hearken back to the time when the Creator's original calendar was known by the entire human race: Septem = seventh, Octo = eighth, Novem = ninth, Decem = tenth. Although December is the 12th Roman month, it still stands in the approximate position of the tenth (Decem) biblical month.

Constantine's Changes

Pontiff Constantine updated the Julian calendar by incorporating the festivals of pagan deities into the new "Christian" celebrations. The day of the birth of Tammuz, who was believed to be the re-incarnated Nimrod, on the winter solstice (originally December 25) was now said to be the birthday of Christ. The day of the re-incarnation of Nimrod's wife as Easter, the queen of heaven and goddess of sexual desire, which was celebrated on the sun-day after vernal equinox, also became a "holy day" on Constantine's religious calendar.

The Roman day begins the same time as it did in ancient Babylon—at midnight—the mathematical moment the sun is on the opposite side of the earth. In the Bible the days begin at sundown (the evening of the previous "day"). The Roman week begins at midnight at the end of the seventh day. Instead of retaining its biblical numbering as the first day, this day was renamed "Deis Solis," or "Sun Day," the day that the sun god was to be worshiped. Pontifex Constantine commanded that everyone rest on "the venerable day of the sun," and that everyone who celebrated the Sabbath or any of the feasts of the Jews would be "cut off."[1]

So not only did Constantine adapt Christian meanings to pagan holidays, but he also forbade Christians or anyone else in the empire from observing the Sabbath or any of the Jewish observances! If Constantine had been scripturally literate, he would have known that these appointed times were not the feasts of the Jews, but rather the feasts of YHVH (Jehovah), which he was demeaning and negating!

> ...and shall wear out the saints of the Most High, and think to change times... (Daniel 7:25).

The Biblical Calendar

The Creator's calendar, or biblical calendar, was the reckoning of time in the Garden of Eden. Each day begins at sunset; each week begins at the sunset at the end of the Sabbath; and each month begins with the sighting of the first sliver of the new moon. The beginning of the year is determined at the new moon when the barley crop in Israel has reached the stage of maturity referred to as "Aviv." This was Israel's national calendar from the time of the constitution at Mount Sinai until long after the dispersion by Rome in the first century. It was the reckoning by which all the feasts of the Lord were conducted during the first and second temple periods, and it was the exact schedule on which the Jewish followers of Jesus continued to keep the feasts.

This is the simplest calendar by which the appointed times of our Creator have always been reckoned and observed. This reckoning of time can be understood by the smallest child and accurately determined by illiterate herdsman. God never changed this calendar. He never changes. As long as we follow His method of making the days, weeks, months, years, sabbath years, jubilee years, and millennia, we won't be ignorant of His times and His seasons.

Chapter 10

ANTI-SEMITISM CONTINUES—ADOLF HITLER AND MARTIN LUTHER

Many of the anti-Semitic teachings that became popular in the first centuries of the Church continued to impact the Church throughout the medieval time period and even up to our present era.

Adolf Hitler

In 1924 at a Christian gathering in Berlin, Adolf Hitler, a professed Christian, stood before thousands of professed Christians and said:

> I believe that today I am acting in accordance with the will of Almighty God. As I announce the most important work that Christians could undertake and that is to be against the Jews and get rid of them once and for all. We are doing the work of the Lord and let's get on with it.[1]

Hitler continued:

> Martin Luther has been the greatest encouragement of my life. Luther was a great man. He was a giant. Within one blow he heralded the coming of the new dawn and the new age. He saw clearly that the Jews need to be destroyed and we're only beginning to see that we need to carry this work on.[2]

He received a standing ovation. Four centuries prior to Hitler, the Christian reformer Martin Luther had preached his last sermon avidly against the Jews and then died four days later.[3] Hitler followed Luther's treatise on how to exterminate the Jews to the letter. Indeed, at his Nuremberg trial, Nazi leader Julius Streicher stated, "I have never said anything that Martin Luther did not say."[4]

Luther's first known comment on the Jews is in a letter written to Reverend Spalatin in 1514:

> Conversion of the Jews will be the work of God alone operating from within, and not of man working—or rather playing—from without. If these offences be taken away, worse will follow. For they are thus given over by the wrath of God to reprobation, that they may become incorrigible, as Ecclesiastes says, for everyone who is incorrigible is rendered worse rather than better by correction.

Shortly before his death on February 18, 1546, Luther preached four sermons in Eisleben. In his second-to-last sermon, he appended what he called his "final warning" against the Jews. The main point of this short work is that authorities who could expel the Jews from their lands should do so if they would not convert to Christianity. Otherwise, Luther indicated, such authorities would make themselves "partners in another's sins."[5]

Paganism in Today's Church

The influence of the mixing between Christianity and paganism that first took place during the Roman Empire has become a major part of how we do church! As we have seen, this anti-Semitism caused the Church to separate itself from the feasts of the Lord and to introduce a whole new set of "holy" days based on things adopted from pagan roots.

The terms *pagan* and *heathen* are traditionally used to define non-Jewish/non-Christian people. Instead of holding to a monotheistic (one

God) belief system, most pagans/heathens worshiped many gods, primarily those from ancient Babylonian, Egyptian, Greek, or Roman mythology.

Jesus said:

> *Thus you are nullifying and making void and of no effect [the authority of] the Word of God through your tradition, which you [in turn] hand on. And many things of this kind you are doing* (Mark 7:13 AMP).

Jesus was saying that when people come up with their own traditions they ultimately become more important to them than the ones God tells them to follow. This is quite clear in the fact that human-made holidays such as Christmas and Easter are very important to most of the Christians in the world, yet very few Christians observe the biblical feasts that God repeatedly told us to observe as an everlasting ordinance through all generations.

> *And this day shall be unto you for a memorial; and ye shall keep it a feast to the LORD throughout your generations; ye shall keep it a feast by an ordinance for ever* (Exodus 12:14).

I have heard every reason why we as Christians do not observe the Lord's feast days. My response is always the same: If we say that we love God and we want to follow His Word, why wouldn't we observe His appointed times? If God is throwing a party at different times of the year and has promised to show up in a special way, then why wouldn't we be there? Instead, we do our own thing that is steeped in paganism, and we don't think it is out of sync with God.

DIVIDED BETWEEN TWO OPINIONS

Researching many of the traditions that we observe in the Church is a real eye-opener. Once I realized what the Christmas tree represents, I was upset that we have allowed them to be in our churches and even on our pulpits for so long. The tree originated from long-practiced pagan celebrations, yet we don't have a problem with putting them in our churches. If you didn't know this, I don't believe that God will judge you for it; but once you know, you should act accordingly.

Many people will say that a Christmas tree is no big deal and that they are not looking at the tree as a means of worship. I am not saying that Christians are worshiping trees; what I am saying is that God clearly says that we should not have any symbols relating to worship of other gods in His house.

This subject was why the big showdown took place with Elijah and Ahab in First Kings chapter 18. Elijah didn't just say that Ahab had turned God's people away from Him; Elijah rebuked Ahab because he allowed a mixing and matching of worship. God's people had true worship symbols in the temple, and they also had trees decorated in the temple as a means of worshiping Baal. That is why Elijah told Israel to make up their mind and decide who they would worship.

> *And Elijah came unto all the people, and said, how long halt ye between two opinions? if the LORD be God, follow Him: but if Baal, then follow him. And the people answered him not a word* (1 Kings 18:21).

The first commandment is that we do not have any other gods *beside* God (see Deut. 5:7). God didn't even want the symbols of worshiping other gods in His house!

Chapter 11

THE SEVEN ANNUAL FEAST DAYS

As mentioned in the Introduction, when I first attended a Messianic Passover seder (feast) I felt such a peace and a joy come over me. It was almost like searching for something for many years and finally finding it. I knew without a doubt that it was a God thing. I then began to search the Scriptures to find out when God told us to stop keeping His feasts. Instead of finding the stopping point of the feasts, I found the exact opposite. I found words like *ordinance* and *forever*. The Lord tells us to keep these feasts *"throughout your generations"* (see Lev. 23:31,41). These days are very important to God.

During the time of great revivals in Israel, one of the first things that the kings did was to re-implement the feast days. It is very clear to me that God never desired for us not to keep the feasts. The closer we get to God, the more we should love what He loves and hate what He hates. That is why Jesus prayed that we become one as He and the Father are one (see John 17:21-22). Jesus walked in complete agreement with the Father because what the Father said, He said, and what the Father liked, He liked, and what the Father disliked, He disliked as well! If you love Him, then you must love His ways, which include His holy days and His feast days.

As with all my teachings, I do not encourage observance of the feasts to cause you to feel condemnation. I do what I do to provoke God's people to a deeper relationship with Him. We receive such a depth of understanding from following God's feast days. It brings us into a closer fellowship with Him.

The enemy knows this, which is why he wants us to believe that they are no longer valid. The devil wants us to feel weird or funny for wanting to observe these days. He wants us to think that the feasts belonged to the Jews and since we are not Jews we should not observe them. I want to be very clear that these feasts belong to the Lord, not the Jews. As a matter of fact, they belong to anyone who truly loves the Lord and who wants to get closer to Him.

THE APPOINTED TIMES OF THE LORD

There are seven annual feasts (appointed times) of God that the Bible tells us to observe. These feasts are a type and shadow of God's yearly cycle that brings us closer to Him. The Bible tells us that we are to keep these appointed times as an ordinance (law) forever through all our generations.

> *These are the feasts of the LORD, even holy convocations, which ye shall proclaim in their seasons* (Leviticus 23:4).

1. Passover

> *In the fourteenth day of the first month at even is the LORD's Passover* (Leviticus 23:5; see also Exodus 12:14; 1 Corinthians 5: 7-8).

Passover celebrates God's deliverance of His people from bondage and slavery. In the Old Testament, God's people were celebrating the time when they were rescued from the slavery of Egypt. This was a type and a shadow of the New Covenant when the Lamb who was slain became the sacrifice that rescued believers from the bondage of sin and death.

When we celebrate Passover, we are celebrating Jesus becoming the sacrifice for His people, thereby delivering us from the bondage of sin and death. We are no longer in slavery and bondage because the blood of the Lamb that causes the "angel of death" to pass over us.

When was the last time you went to a Passover Day parade?

2. The Feast of Unleavened Bread

And on the fifteenth day of the same month is the feast of unleavened bread unto the LORD: seven days ye must eat unleavened bread (Leviticus 23:6).

Leaven represents sin. During this season we are to look to remove anything from our lives that does not line up with the Word of God. Because we have been saved from the bondage of sin, this feast is meant to encourage us to remove anything from our lives that is contrary to God's laws. Any unconfessed sins must be confessed and removed.

3. The Feast of Firstfruits

Ye shall bring out of your habitations two wave loaves of two tenth deals; they shall be of fine flour; they shall be baken with leaven; they are the firstfruits unto the LORD (Leviticus 23:17).

The Bible calls Jesus the firstfruits of all creation (see 1 Cor. 15:20). This feast acknowledges the resurrection of Jesus, and it is also a promise for all Christians who have eternal life that we will be resurrected like Jesus and live forever with Him. We need to demonstrate the joy that we have—because He is resurrected, we **know** that we have eternal life.

The two sheaves represent both Jew and Gentile being presented by the priest to the Father. The High Priest (Jesus) presents us before the Father, and because of His sacrifice, we are acceptable in the eyes of the Lord.

We are also to understand that since God gave His best, we are to do the same!

4. The Feast of Pentecost

The first Pentecost happened 50 days after the day that God delivered His people from the bondage of Egypt. At that time, He brought His people to Mount Sinai and there He made covenant with them. This is what we see here in the book of Exodus.

> And it came to pass on the third day in the morning, that there were thunders and lightnings, and a thick cloud upon the mount, and the voice of the trumpet exceeding loud; so that all the people that was in the camp trembled. And Moses brought forth the people out of the camp to meet with God; and they stood at the nether part of the mount. And mount Sinai was altogether on a smoke, because the LORD descended upon it in fire: and the smoke thereof ascended as the smoke of a furnace, and the whole mount quaked greatly. And when the voice of the trumpet sounded long, and waxed louder and louder, Moses spake, and God answered him by a voice. And the LORD came down upon mount Sinai, on the top of the mount: and the LORD called Moses up to the top of the mount; and Moses went up (Exodus 19:16-20).

> Even unto the morrow after the seventh Sabbath shall ye number fifty days; and ye shall offer a new meat offering unto the LORD (Leviticus 23:16).

> And when the day of Pentecost was fully come... (Acts 2:1).

Pentecost is about open heavens and covenant. The first Pentecost happened 50 days after God delivered Israel from bondage in Egypt.

God opened the heavens and gave His people the first covenant through Moses. The covenant was implemented through the stone tablets of the Ten Commandments and the sacrifice of an animal.

In the New Testament, 50 days after Jesus was crucified, the heavens were opened, and the Holy Spirit was released into the hearts of God's people. Therefore, the New Covenant was implemented. The blood of the New Covenant was the blood of Jesus, the Messiah.

5. *The Feast of Trumpets (Rosh Hashanah)*

> *Speak unto the children of Israel, saying, In the seventh month, in the first day of the month, shall ye have a sabbath, a memorial of blowing of trumpets, an holy convocation* (Leviticus 23:24).

This is a wake-up call to prepare God's people. Traditionally on the Feast of Trumpets the Jews seek to make peace with others so that then they can enter into deep fellowship with the Lord.

When we observe the Feast of Trumpets, it is to prepare us for the soon-coming King. We are to prepare ourselves for eternal fellowship with God. Just like Israel had to get herself ready for the day of fellowship with God, we are to do the same. This is a season of self-reflecting and making ourselves ready to go into the presence of the Lord. The Scriptures demonstrate this when they tell us to first make peace with our brothers and sisters before we can have peace with the Lord:

> *Therefore if thou bring thy gift to the altar, and there rememberest that thy brother hath ought against thee; leave there thy gift before the altar, and go thy way; first be reconciled to thy brother, and then come and offer thy gift* (Matthew 5:23-24).

The fulfillment of this day is when the Lord comes to redeem us once and for all eternity. He will bring judgment to the ungodly and bring eternal joy to all those who obeyed the Gospel.

> *For the Lord Himself shall descend from heaven with a shout, with the voice of the archangel, and with the trump of God: and the dead in Christ shall rise first: Then we which are alive and remain shall be caught up together with them in the clouds, to meet the Lord in the air: and so shall we ever be with the Lord. Wherefore comfort one another with these words* (1 Thessalonians 4:16-18).

6. *The Day of Atonement (Yom Kippur)*

> *Also on the tenth day of this seventh month there shall be a day of atonement: it shall be an holy convocation unto you; and ye shall afflict your souls, and offer an offering made by fire unto the LORD. And ye shall do no work in that same day: for it is a day of atonement, to make an atonement for you before the LORD your God* (Leviticus 23:27-28).

Atonement is a day of restoration and deeper fellowship with the Lord. Leading up to Yom Kippur, God's people were told to make things right with their neighbors in order to move into a deeper relationship with the Father.

We know that under the Old Covenant, the priest had to go into the presence of God and make an animal sacrifice. This sacrifice would atone (cover) the sins of the people. Because it was only a temporary covering, the priests had to do this every year. Because the sacrifice was an animal, it could not completely and permanently cover the sins of humankind. Only a sinless human could do that completely and eternally. Hebrews chapter 9 gives us the full picture of this.

When Jesus died on Calvary, He fulfilled this sacrifice completely and eternally, which is why He is the only acceptable sacrifice for humankind. Only by accepting this sacrifice are we in right relationship to God. That is what we celebrate now when we observe the Day of Atonement. The word *atonement* can also be understood as "at one ment," the condition of being in unity with God.

The future ramifications of this day are that when Jesus returns, we will be in perfect fellowship with Him for all eternity! We not only celebrate what He has done, but we are in a dress rehearsal for what He is going to do in the near future!

7. The Feast of Tabernacles

> *Speak unto the children of Israel, saying, The fifteenth day of this seventh month shall be the feast of tabernacles for seven days unto the LORD* (Leviticus 23:34).

Tabernacles is about experiencing the glory of the Lord. It is about communing and fellowshipping with Him.

> *And let them make Me a sanctuary; that I may dwell among them. According to all that I shew thee, after the pattern of the tabernacle, and the pattern of all the instruments thereof, even so shall ye make it* (Exodus 25:8-9).

> *And the Word was made flesh, and **dwelt** among us...* (John 1:14).

The word *dwelt* is defined as: "to tent or encamp, that is, (figuratively) to occupy (as a mansion) or (specifically) to reside (as God did in the Tabernacle of old, a symbol for protection and communion):—dwell."[1]

> *...(and we beheld His glory, the glory as of the only Begotten of the Father,) full of grace and truth* (John 1:14).

I believe the Feast of Tabernacles was taking place at the time when Jesus was born in the flesh. It is a celebration of God coming to dwell among His people.

When we understand the completeness of God and His Word, we realize that nothing is wasted. Because God is a God of purpose and infinite wisdom, we see that every part of the Word and commandments of God has a specific and significant meaning behind it. Nothing was wasted. The call to those truly seeking truth is to obey and God will give us revelation over time. As with most of the observances, Israel was told to observe the Feast of Tabernacles, and over time the deeper revelation came in the fulfillment of this feast through the Messiah Jesus. Obedience comes first; revelation comes second.

Think about what God said through Tabernacles. He loved His people so much that in the Book of Exodus, He told the people to build temporary dwellings in the wilderness. Every year they were required to do this to remind them of the fact that God had brought them out of bondage and into the land of promise through the desert. Building tents was to not let them forget that God had blessed them with the promise. He then had them build an extra tent for His presence to dwell among His people. The tent that they built for God was exactly like the tents that everyone else lived in.

When Jesus came to Earth, He demonstrated that God loved His people so much that He came to live among them in an earthly tent. The temporary dwelling of His physical body was the same as the dwelling that the people inhabited. The tent in which Jesus lived was temporary in the form that it was in before the resurrection. This is like our bodies, which get old and eventually die. The word *temporary* should be understood to indicate the form it was in, not the body itself. We know that the glorified bodied which Jesus lives in now is the same as the body which all born-again believers will have at the resurrection. Paul reminds us that our earthly bodies are temporary dwellings for our spirits (see 2 Cor. 5). Tabernacles is such a beautiful picture of Jesus coming to Earth and inhabiting a body that is the same as our bodies.

THE IMPORTANCE OF GOD'S APPOINTED TIMES

These appointed times of God are more than just commemorations of events back in Old Testament days. They also are truly significant for New Testament reasons:

- Jesus was crucified during the Passover.

- He was resurrected during Firstfruits.

- He ascended into Heaven and gave us the Holy Spirit during Pentecost.

- He was born during the Feast of Tabernacles.

We will look at this further in Chapter 13. Meanwhile, let's ask ourselves: If these events are that important to God, shouldn't they be to those who love God as well?

> *Purge out therefore the old leaven, that ye may be a new lump, as ye are unleavened. For even Christ our Passover is sacrificed for us: Therefore let us keep the feast, not with old leaven, neither with the leaven of malice and wickedness; but with the unleavened bread of sincerity and truth* (1 Corinthians 5:7-8).

THE FALL FEASTS

Since we have already fulfilled the spring feasts, we are now awaiting the fulfillment of the fall feasts. Will we be ready? The trumpet will blow soon and Jesus is coming back again!

Chapter 12

KEEPING THE SABBATH

THE CYCLES OF GOD

A cycle is something that goes around and moves to a destination. The universe is filled with cycles. Merriam Webster's definition of *cycle* is: "a course or series of events or operations that recur regularly and usually lead back to the starting point; a circular or spiral arrangement." A bicycle is a thing with two (circular) wheels. People use it for transportation. A cycle is a sequence of events that repeat over and over again, for example: the cycle of the seasons. In God's universe, there are cycles of destruction and blessings. In nature there are hurricanes. They go around and around and often lead to terrible devastation. Other cycles of destruction include cycles of addiction, poverty, unbelief, and defeat.

In the Book of Judges, we find the nation of Israel locked into a cycle of sin. The cycle in Judges looks like this:

1. The people rebel against God.

2. God allows their enemies to rise up and oppress them.

3. The people repent and turn back to God.

4. God raises up a deliverer to save them from the enemy.

5. With the enemy oppression broken, they quickly rebel again!

In the Book of Judges, the Israelites went through this cycle seven times! Many people today live their lives in the same manner. During the times of trouble, they seek God, only to forget about Him once they are experiencing prosperity.

Just like the cycles of destruction, God has cycles of blessings. God's economy is different from the world's economy because God's economy deals with sowing and reaping (see Gal. 6:7). When we sow in good soil, we will reap much more than we sow! The result is multiplication and increase. God's cycles of blessings allow us to get closer to Him, to better understand how He works, and to get in line with Him and His Kingdom. God wants to give us increase and to put us into a cycle of victory. At Jericho, God put Israel into a cycle of victory. As they walked in obedience around the city, God brought them into a place of victory (see Josh. 6; Heb. 11:30).

God gave us His cycles in order to break us out of satan's cycle of destruction. God wants to lock us into a cycle of blessing, growth, and increase. As we get in sync with God's cycles, we are spiraled into His pattern of rest and blessing. In the last chapter, we looked at God's annual cycles of feasts. But He instituted another cycle even earlier.

Weekly Cycles

The first cycle is a weekly cycle, which was established by God at the creation of the world. God gave us instructions to work diligently for six days, but then, each week, we are to take the seventh day as a Sabbath, a Shabbat. The word *sabbath* is a Hebrew word that means "intermission," "to take a break." This day is a special day that God set apart to rest and enjoy God's goodness and blessing. (Note: The English word is capitalized when it refers to the Sabbath *day* and not capitalized when it refers to the principle of sabbath *rest*.)

Thus the heavens and the earth were finished, and all the host of them. And on the seventh day God ended His work which He had made; and He rested on the seventh day from all His work which He had made. And God blessed the seventh day, and sanctified it: because that in it He had rested from all His work which God created and made (Genesis 2:1-3).

God Himself sanctified the seventh day. In Mark 2:27-28, Jesus told the Pharisees, "The sabbath was made for man, and not man for the sabbath: Therefore the Son of man is Lord also of the sabbath."

We see God enforcing the sabbath with the children of Israel in the desert. When God fed them directly from Heaven with manna, they were not to gather manna on the Sabbath day. The day before the Sabbath was the only day that His people were to gather enough for two days. Through the Sabbath, God was teaching His children to trust in Him for all their needs and to honor Him for all of His creation.

We also know that keeping the Sabbath day was one of the Ten Commandments (see Exod. 20:8-11). We find no place in the Bible where God tells us that the Ten Commandments are no longer valid. As a matter of fact, the Ten Commandments were *"written with the finger of God"* (see Exod. 31:18), and the Bible also tells us that He didn't add anything. The Bible actually says that after God gave Moses the Ten Commandments, He ceased declaring the Words to Moses, meaning He had completed the task. To me this means His Commandments are complete, and we are not to add or subtract anything from them.

REASONS WHY WE SHOULD OBSERVE THE SABBATH

1. The Sabbath honors God as Creator—it is an act of worship that acknowledges God as Creator.

2.   The Sabbath is a celebration of God's provision—it goes back to God feeding His people with manna from Heaven.

3.   The Sabbath builds our faith—we are depending on Him to meet our needs, even while we are resting in Him.

4.   The Sabbath is a picture of Heaven—it is an indication of how we will rest in the Lord for all eternity.

5.   The Sabbath releases God's blessing—the Bible promises great blessing for those who will receive His gift of the Sabbath.

Also the sons of the stranger, that join themselves to the LORD, to serve Him, and to love the name of the LORD, to be His servants, every one that keepeth the Sabbath from polluting it, and taketh hold of My covenant; even them will I bring to My holy mountain, and make them joyful in My house of prayer: their burnt offerings and their sacrifices shall be accepted upon Mine altar; for Mine house shall be called an house of prayer for all people (Isaiah 56:6-7).

If thou turn away thy foot from the sabbath, from doing thy pleasure on My holy day; and call the sabbath a delight, the holy of the LORD, honorable; and shalt honor Him, not doing thine own ways, nor finding thine own pleasure, nor speaking thine own words: Then shalt thou delight thyself in the LORD; and I will cause thee to ride upon the high places of the earth, and feed thee with the heritage of Jacob thy father: for the mouth of the LORD hath spoken it (Isaiah 58:13-14).

In society, we see many people, especially Christians, who are so tired and burned out that they are really no good for themselves, for their families, or more importantly, for God. God intended us to be well-rested and blessed people who can give 100 percent to God and to our families. We see so many tired, worn-out saints who can only give a portion of their efforts in service to others.

The weekly cycle of resting on the Sabbath is an important one that most Christians overlook. God intended it for us to get recharged and to stay focused on Him and not on ourselves. The Sabbath gives us a chance, every week, to stop and give thanks to Jesus Christ, the Lord of the Sabbath!

Everything that God does and that He requires us to do is for one or more reasons: 1) to bring us in closer relationship to Him, and 2) to build us up and make us better. When we read the Bible with that understanding, it should change how we view Scripture. Instead of looking at Scripture in the New Testament Church as what we don't have to do, we should understand that we benefit from following God's Word. I must not think about what I don't have to do because of God's grace, but about how much better I am when I do what God says to do.

PROVISION FROM HEAVEN

When God first instilled the practice of the Sabbath, He did it by feeding Israel with manna from Heaven. Every day God would literally rain down food for His people to eat. The food was perfect and nourished His people to the extent that none of them ever got sick. He did this to show them that they could and should depend on Him for all their provisions. God's ultimate goal was to have a close and intimate relationship with His people—and what better way than to cause them to look to Him as their source. This practice brings us closer to God as well and helps us develop trust in Him.

During the time of manna in the wilderness, God sent food every day. The manna only lasted one day though, which made them have to look to God for their provision for the day's nourishment ("give us this day our daily bread"). On the sixth day of the week, the day we call Friday, the manna was different. The manna they received on the sixth day lasted for two days. The reason behind this is that on the seventh day (the Sabbath) the Israelites were not allowed to go out and work to gather the food they needed. The Sabbath day was a day of rest commanded by God. On the Sabbath, God's people were to rest and acknowledge the goodness of the Lord in their lives. They also spent time speaking about the great way that God was keeping them and protecting them. Because they were not allowed to travel on that day, the Sabbath strengthened the family structure, bringing father, mother, and children even closer together.

Once Israel entered into the Promised Land, they were still required to observe the Sabbath. They rested from their work, spent time with their families, and spoke of the great things that God continued to do in their lives. In the Books of Deuteronomy and Joshua, God continued to remind them that they were to not let the Word of the Lord depart from their lips and to diligently teach their children about the great things that God does for His people. They were to constantly study the Torah, which strengthened their faith in God while bringing the family unit closer.

You may argue that this is an Old Testament practice that we don't need to observe any more. But there are several problems with this belief. First, the Sabbath was blessed by God once He completed creation. A blessing is attached to the Sabbath day:

> *And God blessed the seventh day, and sanctified* it: *because that in it He had rested from all His work which God created and made* (Genesis 2:3).

God blessed the day, and nowhere in the Bible does it say that God removed that blessing.

Rest

The second part of the command to keep the sabbath is that God's people are required to rest. Rest is important to physical health and to relieve stress. Look at all the tired pastors and other leaders who wear themselves down because they do not take time off to rest. When we rest, we are sending a clear message that we understand that God is our source and our provider. When we work constantly, we send the message that we don't know if God can handle it all, so we better do all that we can!

Therefore I say unto you, Take no thought for your life, what ye shall eat, or what ye shall drink; nor yet for your body, what ye shall put on. Is not the life more than meat, and the body than raiment? Behold the fowls of the air: for they sow not, neither do they reap, nor gather into barns; yet your heavenly Father feedeth them. Are ye not much better than they? Which of you by taking thought can add one cubit unto his stature? And why take ye thought for raiment? Consider the lilies of the field, how they grow; they toil not, neither do they spin: And yet I say unto you, That even Solomon in all his glory was not arrayed like one of these. Wherefore, if God so clothe the grass of the field, which to day is, and to morrow is cast into the oven, shall He not much more clothe you, O ye of little faith? Therefore take no thought, saying, What shall we eat? or, What shall we drink? or, Wherewithal shall we be clothed? (For after all these things do the Gentiles seek:) for your heavenly Father knoweth that ye have need of all these things. But seek ye first the kingdom of God, and His righteousness; and all these things shall be added unto you (Matthew 6:25-33).

Family

One of the most beautiful parts of observing the sabbath is that God requires us to spend time to strengthen our families. When we look at how badly the family structure has broken down, it is no wonder why our society is deteriorating morally. Strong families create strong people, and strong people make strong communities—communities that help to build stronger individuals. That is why the orthodox Jewish community has survived centuries of persecution and attack. God cares about every aspect of our lives; He wants us to prosper in everything we do, especially our families.

Chapter 13

BIBLICAL FEASTS VS.
PAGAN HOLIDAYS

THE ONGOING IMPORTANCE OF THE FEASTS

Making the word of God of none effect through your tradition, which ye have delivered: and many such like things do ye (Mark 7:13).

And honour not his father or his mother, he shall be free. Thus have ye made the commandment of God of none effect by your tradition (Matthew 15:6).

As we saw in Chapter 11, the Word of God outlines the feasts that God has given us to observe. Leviticus 23 lists the biblical feasts. In this portion of Scripture, God tells us, "*...it shall be a statute for ever **throughout your generations** in all your dwellings*" (Lev. 23:14). Most Christians do not take time to observe these biblical feasts that God has told us to observe forever, yet they are often very protective of the pagan festivals that have been adopted into the Church and given Christian meanings.

*And the LORD spake unto Moses, saying, Speak unto the children of Israel, and say unto them, Concerning **the feasts of***

*the LORD, **which ye shall proclaim to be holy convocations**, even these are my feasts. Six days shall work be done:
but the seventh day is the Sabbath of rest, an holy convocation;
ye shall do no work therein: it is the Sabbath of the LORD in
all your dwellings. **These are the feasts of the LORD, even
holy convocations**, which ye shall proclaim in their seasons*
(Leviticus 23:1-4).

The word *feasts* is *mo'adim,* which means "appointed times."[1] God
is telling us that these are appointed times that He has set aside; they
are set by God and not humanity. The word *convocation* comes from
the Hebrew word for "rehearsals." These feasts represent the annual
cycles that God has given us. By observing the biblical feasts, we not
only are being obedient to the Word of God, but we are participating
in the worship of God in a place where God has promised to be. Why
would you not want to be in the place where God has promised He
would be?

The early Church observed the Lord's feasts for the first few hundred
years after Pentecost. It wasn't until the time of Emperor Constantine
that the early Church was separated from its heritage and forbidden to
observe the Lord's feasts. A cycle of blessing and restoration is included
in these feasts. But because the Church today for the most part does not
observe them, we are no longer able to realize this blessing.

The Connection Between the Feasts and Jesus' Life

The first three major events for believers in Jesus—His death, burial,
and resurrection—fell *exactly* on the first three feasts. The symbolism of
the feasts is beyond coincidence!

While Passover was being celebrated—which included the slaying
of an unblemished Lamb—Jesus was being slain on the cross (see 1
Cor. 5:7). Good Friday has been implemented as a replacement to the
Passover. The meal that Jesus ate with His disciples was actually a

Passover seder that the Jews had been keeping for many centuries. At the last meal, Jesus revealed that the Passover they had been keeping for centuries was a prophetic gesture foreshadowing His being offered as a sacrifice for us all. The feast that followed, Unleavened Bread, a picture of sanctification, took place as Jesus was buried. Leaven is representative of sin, of which Jesus had none. The Feast of Firstfruits, which is to be celebrated on the morning *after* the first Sabbath following the Feast of Unleavened Bread (that is, on Sunday) is symbolic of Jesus being the Firstfruits. Jesus was resurrected on "Firstfruits"; that is why He is called first born (Firstfruits) of all creation (see Lev. 23:10-11; 1 Cor. 15:23).

Even more interesting, the next big event for believers was the coming of the Holy Spirit, and it fell **exactly** 50 days after Passover, on what Christians call Pentecost. The word Pentecost means 50; the feast was to take place 50 days after the Passover. The word *Pentecost* is a Greek word, which is why the feast is called Pentecost in the New Testament. The Old Testament calls it Shavuot, which in the Hebrew means "weeks." They had to count seven weeks from the date of Passover.

The symbolism is again obvious, as two loaves of bread are offered unto the Lord in the form of a wave offering, which is a perfect picture of the Old and New Testaments.

The first four major events of the New Testament Church happened on the first four Jewish feasts. Therefore, we can expect that the next big event—the gathering together of God's people—should fall on the next scheduled feast. The next feast happens to be the Feast of Trumpets, or Rosh Hashanah, when God calls His people together for a day of regathering and rejoicing. Again, the symbolism is beyond coincidence.

The question has to be asked: If God placed such a high level of importance on His feast days, then how could we assume they were no longer to be observed or that Jesus "abolished" them?

Emotions and the Promises of God

We have seen how the Church continued in sync with God's feast days for its first few centuries. We have also seen how anti-Semitism caused Constantine and many of the early Church leaders to separate the Church from the will of God. I have made some general statements regarding the influx of paganism that has changed how we worship and acknowledge God.

I want to now get more specific. In the next two chapters, I address the two most important days recognized by Christianity. Those days are Christmas and Easter. Christians all over the world have celebrated these days for decades. There are even some people who only go to church on Christmas and Easter. Most people don't even know the symbolism behind these holidays.

Like most people, I have very fond memories of these days, and my deep faith in the Lord contributed to the good feelings I have attached to them. These feelings are an emotional response to the memories of our past. When I remember Christmas, I think of waking up with butterflies in my stomach and running down the stairs in my house to find out what was under the Christmas tree. I also think about Christmas carols and Christmas cookies. On Easter, I remember getting a sharp new Easter suit and the church being crowded with all the visitors and families coming to celebrate the death, burial, and resurrection of Jesus Christ.

Unfortunately, however, for many of us these emotional memories have hindered us from getting to the deeper things that God has for us. No matter how good we have felt during very spiritual Christmas and Easter celebrations, I guarantee that when we align with what God's Word says, He will take us to deeper depths in Him than we could ever imagine. Remember what the apostle Paul wrote in First Corinthians 2:9: "...*Eye hath not seen, nor ear heard, neither have entered into the heart of man, the things which God hath prepared for them that love Him.*"

I joyfully share these things as I beseech the Body of Christ to turn away from the pagan-based celebrations that we have partaken in for so long and turn back to the beautiful feasts of the Lord. Jesus has promised us that He will meet us during these appointed times in a very special way, and I know that in the upcoming years we are going to see a supernatural manifestation of God the likes of which we have never seen.

A WORD ABOUT HALLOWEEN

I first came across the study of Christmas and Easter while I was doing research about Halloween, also known as *Samhain*. I was preparing a message on why Christians should not participate in Halloween parties, trick or treating, and the like. I found a Wiccan Website that spoke about the season of Samhain and its roots. Wicca is a pagan religion and a type of witchcraft:

> Wicca (pronounced ['wikə]) is a Neopagan religion and a form of modern witchcraft. It is often referred to as Witchcraft or the Craft by its adherents, who are known as Wiccans or Witches. Its disputed origins lie in England in the early 20th century, though it was first popularized during the 1950s by Gerald Gardner, a retired British civil servant, who at the time called it the "witch cult" and "witchcraft", and its adherents "the Wicca." From the 1960s the name of the religion was normalized to "Wicca."[2]

The original traditions surrounding Halloween all stemmed from paganism and were actual things that were done, not just pretend "tricks" or play acting. The pagans really used different means to torture and murder people. Actual human sacrifices take place during the time of Samhain. Halloween and its practices were performed as an act of worship to the devil and his demonic forces. Just as God requires His people to worship Him, the devil does the same. Most biblically sound Christians should recognize that Halloween is something that we should not participate in. The Bible tells us that we should not take on the customs of those who practice these types of things.

The ironic thing about this is that while I was doing the research about Halloween, I came across information about Christmas and Easter also. As I delved deeper into the information, the Wiccan site began talking about the season of Yule. The site had a side note that mockingly discussed how Christians have adopted their pagan celebrations and attached Christian meanings to them. I was shocked to say the least. These pagan practices have been around for centuries. Paganism is an ancient religion. It is believed to be one of several false religions that originated in the ancient city of Babel mentioned in Genesis chapter 11. This caused me to check many other sources, and to my dismay, they all agreed about the heathen roots of the observance that we call Christmas.

Lack of Knowledge

I wondered why Bible-believing Christians would continue to allow pagan practices in the house of God. Most of it is tradition, while even more of it is due to lack of knowledge. The Bible says that God's people perish for the lack of knowledge (see Hos. 4:6). I understand that many Christians are not aware of these facts—I was one of them. Those who do know the truth must realize that God expects us to change our traditions once we know that they contradict the Word of God.

God is doing a new thing. Actually, it is not new; it is just a reconnecting to what He intended in the first place. God is revealing to us the true worship of Him and the way He intended for us to do it. Jesus said that the time will come when the true worshipers will worship Him in spirit and in truth (see John 4:23).

Chapter 14

WHAT'S WRONG WITH CHRISTMAS?

Christmas is the time of year when we celebrate the birth of our Lord and Savior, Jesus Christ. Most of us have some very pleasant thoughts of waking up Christmas morning to find gifts under the Christmas tree. Many of us attach some very pleasant thoughts to the celebration of Christmas, but do we really know why we do what we do? Do we know what this celebration really means? We must believe that what we do in the natural has spiritual ramifications. It is important that we understand the background and the original intent of the observances that we participate in.

Holiness and Truth

Hanging on to these pagan practices limits the movement of the Holy Spirit within our lives and within the Body as a whole. God is looking for us to worship Him in Spirit and in truth. We must also worship Him in the spirit of holiness, which means without any trace of anything evil. No matter how much we feel the presence of the Lord when we participate in these celebrations, God has something greater and more fulfilling for us. We experience God's glory in a greater way by going back to what He intended us to observe—His feast days.

This information regarding the celebrations and the different traditions surrounding Christmas is information that can be found in many different places. The History Channel has much information about this as well as most encyclopedias. I encourage you to seek these things out for yourself. Don't just take my word for it.

However, once you find out that these things are true, you have an obligation to act upon the truth. God requires that His people walk in truth. We are made free by knowing the truth and by walking in agreement with the living Word of God.

Celebrating Jesus' Birthday

I recently had a conversation with a pastor who did not understand why I do not celebrate Christmas. His first question was, "Don't you want to celebrate Jesus' birthday?" My response was, "Yes and no." First, the Bible does not directly tell us when Jesus was born. As you will see, we know the season in which He was born, but not the actual date. Think about the fact that God gave very specific dates for the observances for Passover and the other feasts, yet we don't have the specific date of the birth of the Messiah.

Jesus told us that we are to celebrate His death and resurrection, but He is silent about celebrating His birth. Jesus told us to observe the Passover (we have traditionally known it as communion), which is celebrating the death of Jesus. He said that as often as we observe this we are declaring that He died for our sins and has given us the New Covenant. All of us have been born, but only one man died and then was resurrected to save all of humanity.

The second fact is that we actually do celebrate the birth of the Messiah when we observe the Lord's feast days. The Feast of Tabernacles is the time when we celebrate the Word that became flesh and dwelt among us (see John 1). The Feast of Tabernacles is the season when God required Israel to build a tent for God's presence to dwell in. Paul then reminded us that our bodies are tabernacles that God lives inside (see 1 Cor. 3:16). The Word became flesh and lived among us as the Messiah who took on a human body like ours to live among His people.

This is one of the many challenges that God places before us to examine our hearts. As I stated, Christmas has become an emotional thing that we have attached a godly meaning to. But the question we must ask ourselves is, are we celebrating Jesus' birthday for God or for us? If we are doing it for God, then shouldn't we do it the way God told us to? We do not honor God by doing our own thing and dictating to God that He must accept it. We only truly honor God by offering our worship based on His expectation of how He wants us to worship Him.

Obedience Is Better Than Sacrifice

God has a set of appointed times that He told us to observe. Humankind has replaced the Lord's feast days with our own traditions. Which ones we seek to fulfill will ultimately demonstrate where our hearts are. When we choose to do our own thing over God's commands, then we nullify God's Word. Jesus said the traditions of people make the Word of God of no effect (see Mark 7:13).

A clear example of this is King Saul, who became the first king of Israel. During the battles against the Amorites, God gave a clear commandment that Saul was to destroy all the people and all the cattle that were a part of the Amorite camp. Saul disobeyed God and did not kill the king of the Amorites and kept some of the best cattle. God sent the prophet Samuel to correct Saul. Saul's response was that he decided to keep the best cattle so that he could use them to worship God. In First Samuel 15:19-23, we see this story unfold, and in verse 21 Saul states that they kept the best of the spoils *"to sacrifice unto the LORD thy God in Gilgal."* Saul was telling Samuel that he disobeyed God so that he could worship God his own way.

Samuel's correction is one that we as believers must heed. Samuel tells Saul that *"to obey is better than sacrifice"* (verse 22). We honor God by being obedient and worshiping Him His way. It does not please God when we disobey Him and come up with our own way of giving sacrifices to Him. Obedience to God's Word is the greatest form of worship we can offer Him. In order to truly please God, our first step is obedience to His Word.

That being said, let us look at the symbolic meanings behind the celebration that we have attached to the birth of our Lord Jesus Christ. After looking at their original meanings, I want you to really think about whether or not they honor Jesus. Remember, the Church's first function is to honor God by our actions here on the Earth. That is why we are called after His name.

The Date—December 25

The Scriptures don't give us a date for Jesus' birth. They also never mention any celebration honoring the anniversary of His birth.

The date December 25 comes from pagan midwinter festivals, which were based on myths about gods and goddesses and took place on or near the shortest day of the year. The midwinter date of the Roman festivals of Saturnalia and Dies Natalis Solis Invicti, which translates to the birth of the unconquered sun, was December 25, as set by Emperor Aurelian in A.D. 274. The cult of Sol, the sun god, originated with the Etruscan civilization hundreds of years before the Roman era. In 10 B.C., the Emperor Augustus replaced Sol with Apollo, a Greek god. Apollo was replaced by Mithras, a Persian god from the sixth century B.C. December 25 was the birthday of both sun gods, Mithras and Sol. Egypt's sun god, Osiris, was said to have been murdered by his brother Set and restored to life by Isis on December 25.

Four hundred years after Jesus was born, Church leaders assigned His birthday to the same date as Saturnalia and the Sol celebrations.

In A.D. 360, Constantine, not the Bible, named December 25 as Jesus' birthday. In 1582, Pope Gregory corrected Emperor Julian's Roman calendar consisting of 364 & 1/4 days. In the 16th century the calendar was shortened by 10 days. Britain didn't accept the new calendar until 1751. The lost days now totaled eleven. These intercalary (lost) days had been used to honor the gods in Egypt and the classical world. Now they were also used to honor saints. The 12 days of the Solstice Festival were made part of the festival of Christmas by the Council of Tours in A.D. 560. Christmas day was now the birthday of Mithras, Attis, Aion, Horus, Dionysus, the Unconquered Sun, and Jesus.

Didn't the angels celebrate His birth, bringing tidings of great joy? The angels were sent from God to announce the Messiah's arrival, not to announce the beginning of a yearly festival, and more specifically, not to include Him in midwinter solstice rites.

The Word Christmas

Let it be noted that most people think that the word *Christmas* means "the birth of Christ." By definition, it means "death of Christ." We see this in the *World Book Encyclopedia*, the *Catholic Encyclopedia*, and a book entitled *The Mass in Slow Motion*.[1]

The *World Book Encyclopedia* defines *Christmas* as follows: "The word Christmas comes from 'Cristes Maesse,' an early English phrase that means 'Mass of Christ.'" It is interesting to note that the word *Mass,* as used by the Roman Catholics, has traditionally been rejected by the so-called Protestants, such as Lutherans, Baptists, Methodists, Presbyterians, and Pentecostals and so on.

The word *mass* is strictly a Catholic word and thus, so is "Christ-Mass." The word *mass* in religious usage means a "death sacrifice." The mass is the death sacrifice, and the "host" is the victim. This is official Roman Catholic doctrine, and "Christmas" is a word invented by the

Catholic Church. The impact of this fact is horrifying and shocking, for when the millions of people are saying, "Merry Christmas," they are literally saying "Merry death of Christ"! Consider what you are saying when you say "Merry Christmas." In essence, the mass is the ceremonial slaying of Jesus Christ over and over again, followed by the eating of His flesh and the drinking of His blood.

The Christmas Tree

The pagan custom of decorating trees was being practiced hundreds of years before Jesus ever walked the Earth. The Bible even mentions this practice in the Book of Jeremiah:

> *Thus saith the LORD, Learn not the way of the heathen, and be not dismayed at the signs of heaven; for the heathen are dismayed at them. For the customs of the people are vain: for one cutteth a tree out of the forest, the work of the hands of the workman, with the axe. They deck it with silver and with gold; they fasten it with nails and with hammers that it move not. They are upright as the palm tree, but speak not: they must needs be borne, because they cannot go. Be not afraid of them; for they cannot do evil, neither also is it in them to do good* (Jeremiah 10:2-5).

What does this represent?

Jeremiah 10 is referring to a pagan practice that was taking place for many years prior to Jesus' birth. The Lord was warning the prophet not to let His people participate in these pagan practices. The first "Christmas tree" is attributed to the mythical Phrygian, Attis, who was the son of Cybele, the great mother goddess of Rome. According to the legend, Cybele had a forbidden love for Attis and drove him mad. He castrated himself under a pine tree. The tree became a solstice symbol of everlasting life that was decorated and then cut down.[2]

The Giving of Gifts

The pagan festival of Saturnalia honored Saturn, the Roman god of agriculture and time. The Latin *satus* means "to sow." This festival lasted for seven days, December 17 to 24. The practice of giving gifts came from this festival. Masters served slaves and wore *pillius* (a badge of freedom). Law courts and schools closed. Everyone feasted, gambled, and drank. The festival started with the sacrificium publicum. A young pig was sacrificed in Saturn's temple in the Forum. Wax candles called cerei, symbols of the eternal light, and terra cotta dolls called signillaria, symbols of human sacrifice to the midwinter gods, were exchanged as gifts. Halls were decked with laurel garlands and candlelit green trees.

Didn't the wise men bring Jesus gifts? Yes. The gifts were gold, to be used to purchase Jesus' tomb, and frankincense and myrrh to anoint His body for burial. They were gifts to honor the sacrifice for salvation that He would make, not childish presents.

Santa Claus

In the first historical accounts, shamans climbed trees and brought back "gifts," which were messages from the spirits for the year to come concerning the turning seasons and the fate of the world. *Webster's Dictionary* defines *Shaman* as: "a priest or priestess who uses magic for the purpose of curing the sick, divining the hidden, and controlling events." Their sacks were a bag of tricks. Northern shamans used sleigh bells to scare unfriendly spirits as they entered the spirit world. Their robes were red, linking them to earth, fire, and light. Shamans climbed through a smoke hole in a tent, jingling bells and carrying a red, painted, wood reindeer. They then climbed an evergreen beside the tent. The evergreen was the cosmic tree, and its axial pole connected Heaven and Earth. From the tree top they went on a spirit journey to find gifts of fire, life, and the newborn sun.

St. Nicholas was a third-century bishop of Myra, which is located in Lycia, part of modern day Turkey, who gave anonymous gifts to the poor on December 6, children's day, which eventually became joined with the celebration on December 25.

Other Pagan Aspects of the Season

The feasting, decorating, and other traditions that we now associate with Christmas have been around since the beginning of recorded history. Many of the traditions of Christmas started in ancient Mesopotamia: church processions, house-to-house caroling, feasts, parades, gifts, fires, the yule log, and the 12 days of Christmas. All these rites were held in honor of one or more of the many Mesopotamian gods. Yule is attested early in the history of the Germanic peoples; from the 4th century Gothic language it appears in the month name *fruma jiuleis.*

The English historian Bede wrote that the Anglo-Saxon calendar included the months *geola* or *giuli,* corresponding with either modern December or December and January. He gave December 25 as the first day of the heathen year and wrote that the Anglo-Saxons celebrated all night long to honor the Germanic divine "mothers." They began the year with December 25, the day some now celebrate as Christmas; and the very night to which we attach special sanctity, they designated by the heathen term *Mōdraniht,* that is, the mothers' night—a name bestowed, I suspect, on account of the ceremonies they performed while watching this night through.[3]

The 12-Day Winter Festival

The most important god was Marduk. The Mesopotamians believed that when winter came Marduk battled the "monsters of chaos." A New Year festival called Zagmuk, which lasted 12 days, was held to help Marduk. The king went to Marduk's temple to swear his faithfulness. The king was supposed to die and go to help Marduk battle. The people saved their king by dressing a criminal in royal robes and giving him a king's privileges and respect. The criminal was stripped and killed at the end of the festival, sparing the king's life.

This practice was adapted by other cultures. The Greeks held a festival to help the god Kronos battle Zeus and the Titans, and ancient Europeans held solstice rituals and festivals to help the sun to return.

Human Sacrifice

In Rome's eastern provinces, a mock "king of chaos" was crowned. Lots were cast and the winner took the part of the god Saturn—behaving like a fool, insulting guests, chasing women and girls, and wearing ridiculous clothes. A coin was also put in pudding. The person who got the coin was selected as the mock king. In the more ancient world, the kings were allowed to reign for one year and then they were ritually slaughtered to ensure good luck for the next year and the return of light and fertility.

The Feast of Fools

In medieval times, the Saturnalia festival became the "Feast of Fools," sometimes called the "Feast of Sub-deacons." It was a time of mockery of traditional religious practices. Clergy of the lower orders, canons, and sub-deacons held mock masses. These are parts of the music from the catholic mass. The Mass, a form of sacred musical composition, is a choral composition that sets the invariable portions of the Eucharistic liturgy (principally that of the Roman Catholic Church, the Anglican Communion, and the Lutheran Church) to music. Generally, for a composition to be a full Mass, it must contain the following sections, which together constitute the ordinary of the Eucharist: the Kyrie is the first movement of a setting of the Ordinary of the Mass; the Gloria is a celebratory passage praising God and Christ; the Credo, a setting of the Nicene Creed, is the longest text of a sung Mass.[4]

During the Feast of Fools, priests and clerics wore hideous masks, danced in the choir dressed like women or minstrels, sang filthy songs, and ate black pudding at the horn of the altar while mass was being said. They played dice at the altar, used old shoe soles to make stinking smoke for incense, and ran leaping through the church. Then they drove around town in shabby carts, using indecent gestures and reciting lewd poetry. False bishops, archbishops, and popes wore fool's clothes and carried crosiers and pastoral staffs.

In Beauvais, France, on January 14, a girl with a baby in her arms rode an ass into the cathedral. In the mass, the congregational response was to bray at the Inroit, Kyrie, Gloria, and Credo. At the end of the service, the priest brayed three times instead of saying, "Ite Misa Est" ("the mass has ended"). The people brayed back. In Bourges and Sens it went further. At the Kalends, New Year's Day, the Festum Asinorum, or Feast of the Ass, was held. Kalends is the name the Romans gave to the first day of the month. The Kalends was the day of the new moon. The Feast of the Ass (Latin: *Festum Asinorum* or *asinaria festa*, French: *Fête de l'âne*) was a medieval, Christian feast observed on January 14, celebrating the Flight into Egypt. It was celebrated primarily in France, as a by-product of the Feast of Fools celebrating the donkey-related stories in the Bible, in particular the donkey bearing the Holy Family into Egypt after Jesus' birth.[5] The priest invited the people to come to the altar of Bacchus, the god of wine, and be blessed in wine. Mockery was substituted for the Mass text. The mockery version of the song, which was traditionally sung during this winter festival, goes as such:

> Let us drink: take from us, we beseech thee, Bacchus, all our clothes, that we may be worthy, with naked bodies, to enter the tavern. Unto us all, drink without end. Let the trumpet of the new moon sound and proclaim the celebration of games; in our land to mark our solemn feast day. We have a bishop! The Fool's Bishop! The Lord of the Feast! The Staff of the New Year! Overthrown, overthrown! The Fool's Abbot! Omnia tempus habent! There is time for everything.[6]

This continued far into the 17th century.

This mockery and obscenity are still visible in Mummer's costumes and performances. Greenery is still used to decorate. In England, a man called "the Lord of Misrule" was appointed by royalty and nobles to oversee the Christmas revelry.

Greenery and the Yule Log

Mistletoe was considered a symbol of ever-life because its fruit appeared at the time of the winter solstice. It was sacred to Druid fertility rites. It was cut at the solstice sacrifice ceremony. When dried, it was called "golden bough" and used in magic and for protection. Holly was thought to prevent drunkenness. Dionysus, the god of wine, was believed to have put a dead dancing girl's spirit into it.

The word *yule* means "wheel," and the yule log represents the yearly solstice cycle. It was cut from a fruit tree to make the land fertile and was not allowed to burn through, but kept to rekindle the next year's log.

What Does the Bible Say About Taking on Heathen Practices?

Be ye not unequally yoked together with unbelievers: for what fellowship hath righteousness with unrighteousness? and what communion hath light with darkness? And what concord hath Christ with Belial? or what part hath he that believeth with an infidel? And what agreement hath the temple of God with idols? for ye are the temple of the living God; as God hath said, I will dwell in them, and walk in them; and I will be their God, and they shall be My people. Wherefore come out from among them, and be ye separate, saith the Lord, and touch not the unclean thing; and I will receive you (2 Corinthians 6:14-17).

The cup of blessing which we bless, is it not the communion of the blood of Christ? The bread which we break, is it not the communion of the body of Christ? For we being many are one bread, and one body: for we are all partakers of that one bread. Behold Israel after the flesh: are not they which eat of the sacrifices partakers of the altar? What say I then? that the idol is any thing, or that which is offered in sacrifice to idols is any thing? But I say, that the things which the Gentiles sacrifice, they sacrifice to devils, and not to God: and I would not that ye should have fellowship with devils. Ye cannot drink the cup of the Lord, and the cup of devils: ye cannot be partakers of the Lord's table, and of the table of devils. Do we provoke the Lord to jealousy? are we stronger than He? All things are lawful for me, but all things are not expedient: all things are lawful for me, but all things edify not (1 Corinthians 10:16-23).

And He said unto them, Full well ye reject the commandment of God, that ye may keep your own tradition....Making the word of God of none effect through your tradition, which ye have delivered: and many such like things do ye (Mark 7:9,13).

Pure religion and undefiled before God and the Father is this, To visit the fatherless and widows in their affliction, and to keep himself **unspotted from the world** (James 1:27).

The apostle Paul warned the believers repeatedly to separate themselves from the pagan practices in which the people of their communities were participating. We see that we actually are defiling the holy observances of God by attaching Christian meanings to these ungodly celebrations. Remember, the celebration of Christmas was intentionally implemented as a replacement for the seasons that the Jews were observing. The appointed times observed by the Jews and followed by the first-century Church were commanded by God. The celebrations that replaced them originated from paganism.

Chapter 15

WHAT ABOUT EASTER?

Easter is the other major celebration that the Church has observed for centuries. As you will see, it also is rooted in ungodly practices. The same Emperor Constantine who brought other pagan practices into the Church also looked to replace Passover and the resurrection of Jesus with the practices of his false god worship. This was Constantine's way of meshing the two religions—the Roman worship of many "gods" and Christianity. Constantine did not acknowledge the true and living God, and therefore, obedience to His Word was not important to the emperor. Constantine actually thought of himself as a god and, therefore, believed he had the authority to change the seasons as he saw fit. Easter was not adopted as a "Christian" festival until the fourth century.

The Term Easter

The English word *Easter* is derived from the names *Eostre, Eastre, Astarte,* and *Ashtaroth.* All of these are just variations for *Ashteroth,* the pagan goddess mentioned several times in the Bible. For example, the Book of Judges records that *"the children of Israel did evil again in the sight of the Lord, and served Baalim, and Ashtaroth...and forsook the Lord, and served not Him"* (Judg. 10:6). This same goddess was worshiped by the Chaldeans and Babylonians as Beltis or Ishtar. She was introduced into the British Isles as Astarte by the Druids. So *Easter* is just another name for this goddess known as "The Queen of Heaven."

The apostle Paul actually dealt with this particular false god worship in the Book of Acts. In Acts 19, Demetrius and the other people who had gotten rich from making statues to Diana were about to riot because Paul and the Church caused the people to turn from their pagan practices and turn to worshiping Jesus. Diana was yet another name for this same god. There is truly nothing new under the sun!

Easter is mentioned in Acts 12:1-4:

> *Now about that time Herod the king stretched forth his hands to vex certain of the church. And he killed James the brother of John with the sword. And because he saw it pleased the Jews, he proceeded further to take Peter also. (Then were the days of unleavened bread.) And when he had apprehended him, he put him in prison, and delivered him to four quaternions of soldiers to keep him; intending after* **Easter** *to bring him forth to the people.*

Easter is mentioned here in the King James Version of the Bible because Herod, who was under the authority of Rome, was practicing the pagan holiday of Easter.

The Date

Early Christians celebrated Passover on the 14th day of the first month. A study of the dates on which Easter is celebrated will reveal that the celebration of Easter is not observed in accordance with the prescribed time for the observance of Passover.

The pagans celebrated Easter based on the worship of their gods and pagan observances. In the year 325, the Roman Emperor, Constantine I, assembled the Council of Nicaea. This council unanimously ruled that the Easter festival should be celebrated throughout the Christian world on the first Sunday after the first full moon following the vernal equinox. Because the pagans worshiped the sun, moon, stars, and seasons, all of their observances are based around the change of seasons.

The Pagan Celebration of Easter

The pagan observance of Easter was based on fertility rites. That is where we get Easter eggs and the Easter bunny—they are a sign of fertility. Emperor Constantine and the Roman Catholic Church attached a false Christian meaning to these pagan practices. All these things are historically documented. Even the History Channel verifies the fact that the roots of these Christian holidays stem from paganism. The following passage was taken from the History Channel Website:

Pre-Christian Tradition

Easter, a Christian festival, embodies many pre-Christian traditions. The origin of its name is unknown. Scholars, however, accepting the derivation proposed by the 8th-century English scholar St. Bede, believe it probably comes from *Ēastre,* the Anglo-Saxon name of a Teutonic goddess of spring and fertility, to whom was dedicated a month corresponding to April. Her festival was celebrated on the day of the vernal equinox; traditions associated with the festival survive in the Easter rabbit, a symbol of fertility, and in colored Easter eggs, originally painted with bright colors to represent the sunlight of spring, and used in Easter-egg rolling contests or given as gifts.

Such festivals, and the stories and legends that explain their origin, were common in ancient religions. A Greek legend tells of the return of Persephone, daughter of Demeter, goddess of the earth, from the underworld to the light of day; her return symbolized to the ancient Greeks the resurrection of life in the spring after the desolation of winter. Many ancient peoples

shared similar legends. The Phrygians believed that their om-
nipotent deity went to sleep at the time of the winter solstice,
and they performed ceremonies with music and dancing at the
spring equinox to awaken him.

The Christian festival of Easter probably embodies a number
of converging traditions; most scholars emphasize the original
relation of Easter to the Jewish festival of Passover, or Pesach,
from which is derived Pasch, another name for Easter. The
early Christians, many of whom were of Jewish origin, were
brought up in the Hebrew tradition and regarded Easter as a
new feature of the Passover festival, a commemoration of the
advent of the Messiah as foretold by the prophets.[1]

Easter, Passover, and Firstfruits

I would like to point out several errors in this quote concerning the
meaning of the name and of the observance known as Easter. The assertion that the word *Easter* has anything to do with Passover is incorrect.
Exodus 12 and Leviticus 23 very clearly state that "Passover" is the feast
of the Lord. The Hebrew word for Passover is *pesach* (pronounced *peh'-
sakh*), **not Easter.** Passover is the feast in which Jesus became the sacrifice for all sin.

The Bible states that the Feast of Firstfruits, which takes place three
days after the Passover meal, is the day that our Lord was raised from the
dead. That is why Jesus is referred to as being resurrected and the firstfruits
of those who sleep (see 1 Cor. 15:20). The Bible is very specific about when
Passover is to be observed. This is the Lord's feast that is to be observed "as
a statute forever throughout all our generations," says the Lord.

God's Times vs. Human Traditions

Traditions such as Easter and Christmas that were derived from
paganism and incorporated into the Church under Emperor Constantine

continue to overshadow the observances that God has given us in His Word. Jesus stated in Mark 7:13: *"Making the word of God of none effect through your tradition, which ye have delivered: and many such like things do ye."* As I have shown, the appointed times of God are to be kept forever. I pray that the Lord will open your heart and your mind to seek to please Him by keeping the feasts that are holy unto God.

The apostle Paul tells us:

> *Purge out therefore the old leaven, that ye may be a new lump, as ye are unleavened. For even Christ our Passover is sacrificed for us: Therefore let us keep the feast, not with old leaven, neither with the leaven of malice and wickedness; but with the unleavened bread of sincerity and truth* (1 Corinthians 5: 7-8).

Paul is urging us to look to keep God's seasons and to observe them in the sincere desire to draw closer to Him and to honor Him with the way we worship Him.

Next we will consider how to observe God's laws.

Section III

CHANGING LAWS

"...and think to...change laws..."

Chapter 16

HOW THE ENEMY WANTS
TO CHANGE THE BIBLE

THE PROBLEM

And he shall speak great words against the most High, and shall wear out the saints of the most High, and think to change times and laws: and they shall be given into his hand until a time and times and the dividing of time (Daniel 7:25).

We've seen in Daniel chapter 7 that the antichrist is afflicting and tormenting God's people. He is trying to replace God, and he is blaspheming God and mocking His people. It seems as though the entire world is under his power. The method that he uses to "wear out" the saints is by changing times and laws. In Section II, we discussed the changing of the times of God. In Section III, we will discuss how he looks to change the *laws* of God.

*And he shall speak great words against the most High, and shall **wear out** the saints of the most High, and think to change **times** and **laws:** and they shall be **given into his hand** until a time and times and the dividing of time* (Daniel 7:25).

Wear out = H1080 belâ' (bel-aw') (Chaldee); corresponding to Strong's concordance H1086 (but used only in a mental sense); to afflict:—wear out.

Laws= H1882 תד dâth dawth (Chaldee); corresponding to H1881; decree, law.

Given = derived from the word for "delivered" or "yielded"

Hand = derived from the word for "power" or "authority"[1]

Obviously God had these passages written for a reason. We know the Bible is a book of prophecy. We also know that God gives us His Word to strengthen us and to help us overcome the plans of the devil. When God spells something out for us, it is so that we are not taken off guard and defeated: *"Lest Satan should get an advantage of us: for we are not ignorant of his devices"* (2 Cor. 2:11). God maps out a game plan for us so that we can have victory at all times. I know that the events in the Book of Daniel will come to pass. These events will come to pass only when God's people do not walk in the authority that Jesus made provisions for. God does not want us to be defeated...after all we are His children.

Why Should We Rely on the Bible?

I like to lay the foundation of why we have to rely on the Bible. Why should we believe an ancient book that is thousands of years old? Is the Bible for us in 2011, or was it simply for the people of ancient times? These are questions that we need to ask ourselves when looking for our direction from God.

...You have exalted above all things Your name and Your word (Psalm 138:2 NIV).

God puts His name and His Word above everything else. He is very serious about His reputation. He demonstrates His character by making a covenant through giving us His names and giving us the words of His promises. Because of this character, once His Word is given it cannot be broken.

Billy Graham made this statement about the subject in his book *Storm Warning*:

> In numerous churches the Bible is treated as a collection of fairy tales and fables written by half-educated men of an ancient time. While it offers challenging spiritual myths and wholesome encouragement, some "modern" churches seem to feel that no one should go to the Bible expecting to find absolute truth.
>
> Such teaching is an abomination before God. Nothing could be more destructive to true faith and peace on earth. In the face of such a growing storm, the world desperately needs moorings, and God has given us that anchor in His Word, the Bible.[2]

What Does the Bible Claim to Be?

Let's see what the Bible says about God's Word.

> *Blessed is the man who walks not in the counsel of the ungodly, nor stands in the path of sinners, nor sits in the seat of the scornful; but his **delight is in the law of the Lord**, and in His law he meditates day and night. He shall be like a tree planted by the rivers of water, that brings forth its fruit in its season, whose leaf also shall not wither...* (Psalm 1:1-3 NKJV).
>
> *How can a young man cleanse his way? By taking heed according to Your word. With my whole heart I have sought You; oh,*

let me not wander from Your commandments! **Your word I have hidden in my heart,** *that I might not sin against You!* (Psalm 119:9-11 NKJV).

This is my comfort in my affliction, for Your **word** *has given me life* (Psalm 119:50 NKJV).

The words of the LORD *are pure words: as silver tried in a furnace of earth, purified seven times. Thou shalt keep them, O* LORD; *Thou shalt preserve them from this generation forever* (Psalm 12:6-7).

God has promised to keep His Word intact forever. I believe that God can and will do exactly what He promises to do. If the Church does not get back to relying on the authority of Scripture and training the saints to study and to use the true Word of God, we are doomed. We are easy targets of the enemy!

Forever, O LORD, *Thy word is settled in heaven. Thy faithfulness is unto all generations: Thou hast established the earth, and it abideth. They continue this day according to thine ordinances: for all are Thy servants. Unless Thy law had been my delights, I should then have perished in mine affliction. I will never forget Thy precepts: for with them Thou hast quickened me. I am Thine, save me: for I have sought Thy precepts. The wicked have waited for me to destroy me: but I will consider Thy testimonies. I have seen an end of all perfection: but Thy commandment is exceeding broad* (Psalm 119:89-96).

God has vowed to preserve his Word forever. Do we believe that He is capable of doing this?

The Misconception of Inspired

One of the misconceptions of the Bible is that we can discount the Word by just relegating it to being a book of men's perceptions of God. Second Timothy 3:16 says that *"all Scripture is given by **inspiration** of God."*

By using the English word *inspired,* we lose much from the original Greek interpretation. The English term for *inspired* often is viewed as an emotional thing. I could see a beautiful woman, and it might inspire me to write a song. I could have a happy or a sad experience, and because of that, I may write a poem or a book. That is why it is easy for many people to question the Scriptures or to believe that the Bible is inaccurate. I have even heard people say they believe that the Bible is outdated because the men who wrote it were looking at things from their personal frames of reference. If I believe that the writers of the Bible were simply writing things based on an emotional response, then I can also believe that because times have changed, then maybe what God believes has changed as well.

The Greek word for *inspired* is *theopneustos,* which literally means "God breathed." It comes from the root words *theo* (meaning God) and *pneo-* (meaning to breathe).[3] This tells us that these men were not just writing from their emotional responses, but that God literally breathed these words into their spirits. This makes the Bible much more than just a book of stories.

*We have also a more sure word of prophecy; whereunto ye do well that ye take heed, as unto a light that shineth in a dark place, until the day dawn, and the day star arise in your hearts: Knowing this first, that no prophecy of the Scripture is of any private interpretation. For the prophecy came not in old time by the will of man: but holy men of God spake as they **were moved** by the Holy Ghost (2 Peter 1:19-21).*

The word *moved* comes from the Greek word *pherō* meaning to "be driven" or to be "moved by."[4] It denotes that the Holy Spirit literally wrote through the writers of the Bible.

Peter tells us that the Bible is a sure word of prophecy that was given to all people. It was written by certain authors who were moved by the Holy Ghost. This same Holy Ghost is also known as the Spirit or the *pneuma* (the breath) of God.

The day I realized this was an eye-opener. No longer did I look at the Bible as just some words of wisdom. The words in the Bible were literally breathed into men by God. It is like an implanting of words used by God to get His message through to us. I believe they are supernatural words that have the ability to change and to transform us into God's image.

The amazing thing about all this is that the Bible describes the process of its writing as being similar to the creation of the world. The Holy Spirit was present, and the Word implemented the creation process! Just as God breathed life into Adam and he became a living being, God breathed the words of life into His humble servants so that we can have life and have it more abundantly.

Chapter 17

WHAT DID JESUS SAY
ABOUT THE BIBLE?

THE BIBLE IS ETERNAL

"But it is easier for heaven and earth to pass away than for one stroke of a letter of the Law to fail" (Luke 16:17 NASB). The word here for *law* is the Greek word *nomos*. *Nomos* refers to God's law, also known as the Law of Moses (the Torah).

Jesus said:

> *Think not that I am come to destroy the law, or the prophets: I am not come to destroy, but to fulfil. For verily I say unto you, Till heaven and earth pass, one jot or one tittle shall in no wise pass from the law, till all be fulfilled* (Matthew 5:17-18).

Jesus is making a reference to the Torah, the book of the Law. We can define the Torah as the first five books of the Bible: Genesis, Exodus, Leviticus, Numbers, and Deuteronomy. The Torah is also known as "the Law of Moses" or simply "the Law." When Jesus mentions the Law, this is what He is speaking of.

Jesus says here that Heaven and Earth will cease to exist before the Torah is completely fulfilled. "Jots" and "tittles" were the smallest details of the Hebrew language. They are the same as commas and periods in our modern-day language. Since Heaven and Earth continue to exist, it is safe to say that the Word of God is still intact.

Jesus said that Heaven and Earth will pass away first and that the smallest detail of the Bible will not go away until everything is fulfilled.

> *For I testify unto every man that heareth the words of the prophecy of this book, If any man shall add unto these things, God shall add unto him the plagues that are written in this book: And if any man shall take away from the words of the book of this prophecy, God shall take away his part out of the book of life, and out of the holy city, and from the things which are written in this book* (Revelation 22:18-19).

The Bible Is About Jesus

> *And He said to them, "O foolish men and slow of heart to believe in all that the prophets have spoken! Was it not neces-sary for the Christ to suffer these things and to enter into His glory?" Then beginning with Moses and with all the prophets, He explained to them the things concerning Himself in all the Scriptures* (Luke 24:25-27 NASB).

Moses and *the prophets* here refer to the books written by each—in other words, the Old Testament. Jesus was showing His disciples how the Old Testament was a type and shadow of Himself. When we study the Bible, we are actually confirming the Messiah.

We must realize something about these passages: When Jesus, Paul, and others refer to the Scriptures, they were not talking about the New Testament. The New Testament had not been written during the time that Jesus walked the Earth. During the time of Paul and the other apostles, they were in the process of completing the New Testament. Jesus was letting us know that the Bible in its entirety has a purpose and a benefit for us. That benefit did not cease with the implementation of the New Testament. We will discuss that in more detail as we go forward, but I thought it was important to remind us that *all* Scripture includes both testaments.

There is nothing in the New Testament that was not first talked about in the Old. The New Testament is the revelation of the foundation that God was laying in the Old. There is a saying, the Old Testament has concealed that the New Testament has revealed.

The Bible declares that it is the Word, the Law, the decree, and the commandments of God. Now that you know what the Bible claims and what the words of Jesus say about the Bible, the question is: Do you believe?

Chapter 18

HOW DID WE GET THE BIBLE?

Many intellectuals try to discredit the authenticity of the Bible. Some even try to deny the fact that Jesus ever existed as a man 2,000 years ago. Some critics believe that the Bible has been tampered with and that much of the Bible has been deleted, added to, or corrupted. There is an incredible problem with allowing others to discredit the Holy Bible. If we cannot rely on the Bible as a whole, what parts can we believe? Worse yet, to whom should we turn to give us truth? If we cannot use the Bible as our guide, what can we use?

The evidence against these philosophies is quite clear. No written record, since the beginning of the world, has been maintained in its original form as accurately and for as many years as the Bible. No other human being has had his or her biography preserved as accurately as Jesus Christ. The Bible is considered the most accurate historical document of all time for the reasons we will be discussing.

Is the Bible Accurate?

Critics argue that we should disregard the Bible because it is impossible that our modern versions could match the original texts. But how does this argument stand up to scrutiny? Has the Bible been preserved accurately? Are the Scriptures that we read today the same as the ones originally written so long ago? Has the Bible been changed, or does it constitute the same inspired words written by the prophets and the apostles?

Of course, there are language differences because the Bible was not originally written in English. The Old Testament was written primarily in Hebrew, with a few parts in Aramaic, also known as Chaldean. The New Testament was written in Greek. The Bible wasn't translated into English until the 14th century. But did it change over the many centuries until then?

These are important questions. If it can be shown that the Bible we have today is different from the one God originally inspired, why should we pay attention to it? If we can't trust that it has been accurately translated and preserved, there is little reason to trust that it is indeed God's Word. So it is very important that we see what the historical record shows.

The Preservation of the Old Testament

The Hebrew Bible, what today is called the Old Testament, is far older than the New Testament—having been written between approximately 1446 and 400 b.c., some 25 to 35 centuries ago. Is the version we have today a faithful and accurate rendition of the original? Let's take a look at how it was preserved for us.

The apostle Paul wrote that the oracles of God were committed to the Jewish people (see Rom. 3:2). For centuries they carefully and meticulously preserved their sacred writings. The manuscripts of the Bible that we have today were written by hand long ago, well before the invention of the printing press. The Jewish scribes who made the copies of the Old Testament Scriptures from generation to generation were scrupulously cautious about their copying procedures.

This meticulous care was perpetuated by the Masoretes, a special group of Jewish scribes who were entrusted with making copies of the Hebrew Bible from about a.d. 500 to 900. Their version of the Old

Testament, widely considered the most authoritative, came to be known as the Masoretic Text. Before and during this time, trained copyists followed various meticulous and stringent requirements for making scrolls of their holy books. The Masoretes required that all manuscripts have various word numbering systems. As an example of one test they used, when a new copy was made, they counted the number of words in it. If the copy didn't have the proper count, the manuscript was unusable and buried. Such steps ensured that not a single word could be added to or left out of the Holy Scriptures. Through such steps, the scrolls that formed the Hebrew Bible were copied meticulously, carefully, and accurately, century after century.

The Canon of the Old Testament

About A.D. 90, Jewish elders meeting in the Council at Jamnia, in Judea near the Mediterranean coast, affirmed that the canon (the set of writings acknowledged as being divinely inspired) of the Hebrew Bible was complete and authoritative. While there are some differences in organization between the Hebrew Bible and our Old Testament, the content is nonetheless the same.

The Hebrew Bible combines the text into 22 books while our modern Bibles divide the Old Testament into 39. The differences are due to the fact that books like Joshua and Judges were written on one scroll, thus making them one book by Jewish count, while they appear as separate books in our modern Bibles. Similarly, First and Second Samuel and First and Second Kings all made up one book in Jewish reckoning, as did First and Second Chronicles. All these were divided into multiple books and placed in a different order in our English translations.

The Jewish Council at Jamnia rejected other questionable books, known as the Apocrypha and Pseudepigrapha, as inspired or authoritative. So they are not part of this count or the accepted Hebrew canon. Thus these books are left out of most modern Bibles.

Through the centuries, the Jewish people were very careful to preserve the Old Testament as we have it today. The majority of the manuscripts that we have today of the Old Testament are virtually identical to the copies made by the Masoretes, with very little difference between them.

The Field of Textual Criticism

Textual criticism is the field of study in which experts compare the various manuscripts in existence to one another, seeking to come as close as possible to what the original author wrote. The original manuscripts are called *autographs*, literally "self writings." Today, with the passage of so much time, no autographs, original copies, exist of any of the Old or New Testament books. Over the centuries, minor differences, called *variants,* often make their way into successive copies of handwritten documents, even with the greatest of care by the scribes involved. Textual criticism tries to identify these variations and determine what the original texts said.

After 1455 and Johannes Gutenberg's invention of the first movable, metal, type printing press, the Bible could be printed over and over again with predictable accuracy, so variants no longer were a concern. However, before that time, manuscripts still had variants. Thus the period before 1455 is where textual criticism comes into play.

Because of the strict requirements and few locations where the Old Testament was copied, few variants or versions of the Old Testament ever came into existence. In 1947, the Dead Sea Scrolls were discovered, which consisted primarily of portions of the Old Testament dating mostly from the first century B.C. Because the Dead Sea Scrolls were 1,000 years older than the oldest and most reliable Masoretic Text we have today (the Leningrad Codex, dating to A.D. 1008), scholars thought they might find drastic differences over that long passage of time. But did they?

After years of study, they found that the Dead Sea Scrolls they examined have only a relatively few, minor and insignificant differences from today's Masoretic Text of the Old Testament! Historian Ian Wilson explains:

> These oldest-known biblical texts have one absolutely crucial feature. Although...a thousand years older than the texts previously available in Hebrew, they show just how faithful the texts of our present Bibles are to those from two thousand years ago and how little they have changed over the centuries. Two Isaiah scrolls, for instance, contain the Isaiah text almost exactly as it is in our present-day Bibles...

> Although there are, as we might expect, some minor differences, these are mostly the interchange of a word or the addition or absence of a particular phrase. For example, whereas in present-day Bibles, Isaiah *1:15 ends, "Your hands are covered in blood", one of the Dead Sea pair adds, "and your fingers with crime". Where Isaiah 2:3 of our present-day Bibles reads, "Come, let us go up to the mountain of [the Lord], to the house of the God of Jacob", the Dead Sea Scroll version omits, "to the mountain of [the Lord]".* Such discrepancies are trifling, and there can be no doubt that the biblical books someone stored away so carefully at Qumran two thousand years ago were as close to those we know in our present Hebrew and Old Testament Bibles as makes no difference.[1]

The differences, however, do not imply the Dead Sea Scrolls were correct and the Masoretic Text is incorrect. We should keep in mind that the Dead Sea Scrolls were not necessarily transcribed with the same meticulous preservation practices as those used by the main scribes of the time. Nonetheless, the remarkable discovery of the Dead Sea Scrolls is astounding confirmation that the Old Testament has indeed been accurately preserved for us today.

Number of Ancient Texts

The bibliographical test for reliability of a manuscript is an examination of the textual transmission by which documents reach us. In other words, since we do not have the original documents, how reliable are the copies we have in regard to the number of existing manuscripts (MSS) and the time interval between the original and extant (currently existing) copies.[2]

F.E. Peters states that "on the basis of manuscript tradition alone, the works that made up the Christian New Testament were the most frequently copied and widely circulated books of antiquity."[3] As a result, the fidelity of the New Testament texts rests on a multitude of manuscript evidence. Counting Greek copies alone, the New Testament is preserved in some 5,656 partial and complete manuscript portions that were copied by hand from the second through the 15th centuries.[4]

There now are more than 5,686 known Greek manuscripts of the New Testament. Add at least 9,300 other early versions (MSS), and we have close to, if not more than, 15,000 manuscript copies of portions of the New Testament in existence today. No other document of antiquity even begins to approach such numbers and attestation. In comparison, Homer's Illiad is second, with only 643 manuscripts that still survive. The first complete preserved text of Homer dates from the 13th century.[5]

Sir Fredrick Kenyon, who was the director and principal librarian of the British Museum and second to none in authority for issuing statements about MSS, states that:

> The interval between the dates of original composition and
> the earliest extant evidence becomes so small as to be in fact
> negligible, and the last foundation for any doubt that the

Scriptures have come down to us substantially as they were written has now been removed. Both the authenticity and the general integrity of the books of the New Testament may be regarded as finally established.[6]

Dockery, Matthews, and Sloan, have recently written:

For most of the Biblical text a single reading has been transmitted; elimination of scribal errors and intentional changes leaves only a small percentage of the text about which any questions occur.[7]

They conclude:

It must be said that the amount of time between the original composition and the next surviving manuscript is far less for the New Testament than any other work in Greek literature... Although there are certainly differences in many of the New Testament manuscripts, not one fundamental doctrine of the Christian faith rests on a disputed reading.[8]

The following is a breakdown of the number of surviving manuscripts for the New Testament:

Extant Greek manuscripts:

Unicals	307
Miniscules	2,860
Lectionaries	2,410
Papyri	109
Subtotal	**5,686**

Manuscripts in other languages:

Ethiopic	2,000 plus

Slavic	4,101
Armenian	2,587
Syriac Peshitta	350 plus
Bohairic	100
Arabic	75
Old Latin	50
Anglo Saxon	7
Gothic	6
Sogdian	3
Old Syriac	2
Persian	2
Frankish	1
Subtotal	**9,284**
Total All MSS	**14,970**[9]

To put it plainly, there are more translations of the Bible in various languages that agree with each other and are dated very closely to the time of the events than there are translations of any other text. To believe that we do not have accurate translations of the original writings of the Bible is a misconception. To suggest that every one of these versions had been tampered with would take a conspiracy of unimaginable proportions.

Intellectuals who suggest that we do not have the original writings from the biblical authors are misguided. While we technically don't have the original copies, I believe that historical data proves beyond a reasonable doubt that we in fact do have the true Bible. It was preserved through the many scribes that God ordained to keep it intact. I also believe that if we question the authenticity of the Bible in its current form, we then must question to a much larger extent any historical writing of any event, place, or time in history. To do this would be absurd.

God requires us to know His Word. He has given us His Word as a guide on how to live in this world and how to get closer to Him. To believe that God did not make provision for us to have His Word in the form in which He gave it is to shortchange God. The Bible tells us that we are washed by the Word (see Eph. 5:26). In John 17:17-19, Jesus says that He has "sanctified" us by the Word of God. We will be able to stand up against the great deceptions of satan in the end times only because of the Word being rooted in our souls.

Chapter 19

HAS SATAN CHANGED THE BIBLE?

SATAN'S TACTICS

God provides us with some insight as to the devices that satan will use to afflict and overcome God's people. He gives us that information so that we can effectively fight against the plan of the enemy!

The first mention of satan in the Bible is in Genesis 3:1:

*Now the serpent was more **subtil** than any beast of the field which the LORD God had made. And he said unto the woman, Yea, hath God said, Ye shall not eat of every tree of the garden?*

The two primary things that we see here about satan are that he uses subtlety in deceiving Eve and that his primary weapon against God's people is to twist God's words—using part of the truth to nullify the Word of God! The enemy continues to use subtlety and deception in achieving His goals. Many times he cannot just tell us to turn away from God, but he can place us on a gradual decline that allows us to slowly erode in the things of faith. The gradual loss of our faith in the Bible is more dangerous and a more effective tool of the enemy than to simply come against the Bible. Just allowing for questions of authenticity to arise in regard to the Bible can be the greatest weapon against the Bible. If we can raise questions of doubt of any parts of the Bible, it ultimately allows for the total disregard of the authority of the Bible as being the inspired Word of God.

Bible Stats

The word *Bible* comes from a Latin form of the Greek word *biblia,* which means "little books." The Holy Bible is a collection of 66 books from different authors compiled together. Thirty-nine of the original books kept by ancient Israel in Hebrew are the ones we know today as The Old Testament. The last section of the Bible, known familiarly as The New Testament, is comprised of 27 books or letters written in Greek. The Greek used was not formal Greek, but the conversational Greek spoken at the time of the apostles.

Forty men shared in the writing of the Bible over a span of about 1,600 years, beginning in the time of Moses and ending with the last book written by John. The last book of the Old Testament, Malachi, was written about 443 B.C. The first book of the New Testament, Matthew, was written about A.D. 40, leaving approximately a 500-year gap between the Old and New Testament books.

Number of Books in the Bible	66
Chapters	1,189
Verses	31,101
Words	783,137
Letters	3,566,480
Number of promises given in the Bible	1,260
Commands	6,468
Predictions	over 8,000
Fulfilled prophecy	3,268 verses

The Danger of Tampering With the Word

For I testify unto every man that heareth the words of the prophecy of this book, If any man shall add unto these things, God shall add unto him the plagues that are written in this book: And if any man shall take away from the words of the book of this prophecy, God shall take away his part out of the book of life, and out of the holy city, and from the things which are written in this book (Revelation 22:18-19).

We have to be mindful of anyone who tampers with the Word of God. To change the Word of God and its meaning also changes the power that comes from within the Word of God. When Jesus was tempted in the wilderness, He replied to satan every time with the words, *"It is written."* Because Jesus Christ used the power of the Word, satan had no power to persuade Him to sin.

Many of our modern Bible translations have changed the very meanings of the Word of God. This has taken away the power that exudes from the Word of God. The Holy Spirit comes into agreement with the Word of God in order to activate its power. When we use a translation that changes the meaning, we also take away the power of the Holy Spirit to move on our behalf.

The Need to Have the True Word of God

The Word of God is an important piece of our relationship with God. We cannot separate God from His Word.

In the beginning was the Word, and the Word was with God, and the Word was God (John 1:1).

For there are three that bear record in heaven, the Father, the Word, and the Holy Ghost: and these three are one (1 John 5:7).

The Word is essential to our growth in the Lord:

> *All scripture is given by inspiration of God, and is profitable for doctrine, for reproof, for correction, for instruction in righteousness* (2 Timothy 3:16).

Thus far we have established that: 1) God cares about every detail of His Word, 2) He promised to preserve His Word Himself, and 3) every part of the Bible is given for our benefit!

The Role of the Holy Spirit in Knowing God's Word

> *Nevertheless I tell you the truth; It is expedient for you that I go away: for if I go not away, the Comforter will not come unto you; but if I depart, I will send Him unto you. And when He is come, He will reprove the world of sin, and of righteousness, and of judgment: Of sin, because they believe not on Me; of righteousness, because I go to My Father, and ye see Me no more; of judgment, because the prince of this world is judged. I have yet many things to say unto you, but ye cannot bear them now. Howbeit when He, the Spirit of truth, is come, He will guide you into all truth: for He shall not speak of Himself; but whatsoever He shall hear, that shall He speak: and He will shew you things to come. He shall glorify Me: for He shall receive of Mine, and shall shew it unto you. All things that the Father hath are Mine: therefore said I, that He shall take of Mine, and shall shew it unto you* (John 16:7-15).

The Holy Spirit confirms the Word of God. The Holy Spirit and the Word of God must agree in order for Christians to have power and to overcome the works of the devil. It is only through the revelation of the Holy Spirit that we can truly understand the Word of God. Those with carnal, unsaved minds are unable to comprehend the true Word of God; it is foolishness to them.

But the natural man receiveth not the things of the Spirit of God: for they are foolishness unto him: neither can he know them, because they are spiritually discerned (1 Corinthians 2:14).

We will see in the following chapters how satan has used deception to try to weaken the power of the Word of God and how we truly need the Holy Spirit to protect us from his tactics.

Chapter 20

FROM THE ORIGINAL LANGUAGE TO ENGLISH

Now that we have seen that the original content of the Bible was accurately preserved over the centuries in its original languages, we need to look at another issue—translation. Has the Bible been accurately translated from its original languages into the English versions that we read today?

The Limitations of Translations

Many people will tell you that you have to know Greek and Hebrew in order to fully understand the Scriptures. I disagree with that assertion. However, I do acknowledge that there are some limitations of the Word translated from the original Hebrew and Greek to English. I have found that the English language is not as descriptive and complete as Hebrew or Greek. While we have one word for *love*, for example, the Greek language has several. In Hebrew one word can have the same meaning as an entire sentence in English. Therefore, to get a fuller meaning of the Scriptures, it is good for a person to have an understanding of Greek and Hebrew. It is not a must, but it does help a lot.

So, for all of us who are not fluent in ancient Hebrew and Greek, how do we know which translation to use? In order to answer that question, we need to look at the process of translation and some history of translation of the Scriptures into English.

THE HISTORY OF THE ENGLISH BIBLE

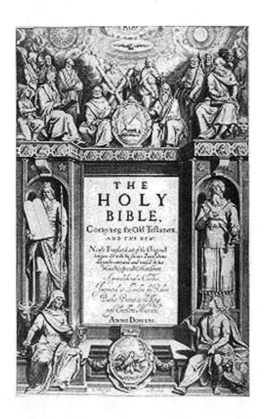

The title page to the 1611 first edition of the Authorized Version Bible by Cornelius Boel shows the apostles Peter and Paul seated centrally above the central text, which is flanked by Moses and Aaron. In the four corners sit Matthew, Mark, Luke and John, authors of the four gospels, with their symbolic animals; the rest of the apostles stand around Peter and Paul.

Early English translations

The followers of John Wycliffe undertook the first complete English translations of the Christian Scriptures in the 15th century. The Wycliffe

Bible pre-dated the printing press, but was circulated widely in manuscript form, often inscribed with a date earlier than 1409 to avoid the legal ban.

In 1525, William Tyndale, an English contemporary of Martin Luther, undertook a translation of the New Testament. Tyndale's translation was the first printed Bible in English. Over the next ten years, Tyndale revised his New Testament in the light of rapidly advancing biblical scholarship and embarked on a translation of the Old Testament. Despite some controversial translation choices, the merits of Tyndale's work and prose style made his translation the ultimate basis for all subsequent renditions into Early Modern English. With these translations lightly edited and adapted by Myles Coverdale, in 1539, Tyndale's New Testament and his incomplete work on the Old Testament became the basis for the Great Bible.

This was the first "authorized version" issued by the Church of England during the reign of King Henry VIII. When Mary I succeeded to the throne in 1553, she returned the Church of England to the communion of the Roman Catholic faith, and many English religious reformers fled the country, some establishing an English-speaking colony at Geneva. Under the leadership of John Calvin, Geneva became the chief international center of Reformed Protestantism and Latin biblical scholarship.

These English expatriates undertook a translation that became known as the Geneva Bible. This translation, dated to 1560, was a revision of Tyndale's Bible and the Great Bible on the basis of the original languages. Soon after Elizabeth I took the throne in 1558, the flaws of both the Great Bible and the Geneva Bible (namely, that the Geneva Bible did not "conform to the ecclesiology and reflect the Episcopal structure of the Church of England and its beliefs about an ordained clergy") became painfully apparent. In 1568, the Church of England responded with the Bishops' Bible, a revision of the Great Bible in the light of the Geneva version.

While officially approved, this new version failed to displace the Geneva translation as the most popular English Bible of the age—in part because the full Bible was only printed in lectern editions of prodigious size and at a cost of several pounds. Accordingly, Elizabethan lay people overwhelmingly read the Bible in the Geneva Version—small editions were available at a relatively low cost. At the same time, there was a substantial clandestine importation of the rival Douay-Rheims New Testament of 1582, undertaken by exiled Roman Catholics. This translation, though still derived from Tyndale, claimed to represent the text of the Latin Vulgate.

In May 1601, King James VI of Scotland attended the General Assembly of the Church of Scotland at St. Columba's Church in Burntisland, Fife, at which proposals were put forward for a new translation of the Bible into English. Two years later, he acceded to the throne of England as King James I of England.

The newly crowned King James convened the Hampton Court Conference in 1604. That gathering proposed a new English version in response to the perceived problems of earlier translations as detected by the Puritan faction of the Church of England.

King James commissioned a committee to translate the Bible based on urging of the Puritans who detected minor problems in the previous English translations. The problems were minor problems and not necessarily doctrinal ones.

Here are three examples of problems the Puritans perceived with the Bishops' and Great Bibles.

First, Galatians 4:25 (from the Bishops' Bible):

> The Greek word susoichei is not well translated as now it is, bordereth neither expressing the force of the word, nor the apostle's sense, nor the situation of the place.

Second, Psalm cv. 28 (from the Great Bible):

"They were not obedient," the original being, *"They were not disobedient."*

Third, Psalm cvi. 30 (also from the Great Bible):

"Then stood up Phinees and prayed," the Hebrew hath, *"executed judgment."*

APPROACHES TO TRANSLATION

Dynamic Versus Formal Equivalence

Dynamic equivalence and formal equivalence are two approaches to translation. Dynamic equivalence (also known as functional equivalence) attempts to convey the thought expressed in a source text (if necessary, at the expense of literalness, original word order, the source text's grammatical voice, and so forth), while formal equivalence attempts to render the text word-for-word (if necessary, at the expense of natural expression in the target language). The two approaches represent emphasis, respectively, on readability and on literal fidelity to the source text. There is, however, in reality no sharp boundary between dynamic and formal equivalence. Broadly, the two represent a spectrum of translation approaches.

The terms *dynamic equivalence* and *formal equivalence* are associated with the translator Eugene Nida and were originally coined to describe ways of translating the Bible, but the two approaches are applicable to any translation.

Theory and Practice

Because dynamic equivalence eschews strict adherence to the grammatical structure of the original text in favor of a more natural rendering in the target language, it is sometimes used when the readability of the translation is more important than the preservation of the original grammatical structure. Thus a novel might be translated with greater use of dynamic equivalence so that it may read well, while in diplomacy or in some business settings, powerful people who do not understand the nature of translation may insist on formal equivalence because they believe that fidelity to the grammatical structure of the language equals greater accuracy.

Formal equivalence is often more goal than reality, if only because one language may contain a word for a concept which has no direct equivalent in another language. In such cases, a more dynamic translation may be used or a neologism may be created in the target language to represent the concept (sometimes by borrowing a word from the source language).

The more the source language differs from the target language, the more difficult it may be to understand a literal translation. On the other hand, formal equivalence can sometimes allow readers familiar with the source language to see how meaning was expressed in the original text, preserving untranslated idioms, rhetorical devices (such as chiastic structures in the Hebrew Bible), and diction.

Bible Translation

The concept of dynamic equivalence, applied to Bible translation, was developed especially by the linguist Eugene A. Nida. Translators of the Bible have taken various approaches in rendering it into English, ranging from an extreme use of formal equivalence, to extreme use of dynamic equivalence.

Selecting Source Text

Another key issue in translating the Bible is selecting the source text. The Bible far predates printing presses, so every book had to be copied by hand for many centuries. Every copy introduced the risk of error. Thus, a key step in performing a translation is to establish what the original text was, typically by comparing extant copies. This process is called textual criticism.

Textual criticism of the Old Testament (Hebrew Bible) centers on the comparison of the manuscript versions of the Masoretic text to early witnesses such as the Septuagint, the Vulgate, the Samaritan Pentateuch, various Syriac texts, and the biblical texts of the Dead Sea Scrolls.

The New Testament has been preserved in more manuscripts than any other ancient work, creating a challenge in handling so many different texts when performing these comparisons. The King James Version (or Authorized Version) was based on the Textus Receptus, an eclectic Greek text prepared by Erasmus based primarily on Byzantine text Greek manuscripts, which make up the majority of existing copies of the New Testament. The majority of New Testament textual critics now favor a text that is Alexandrian in complexion, especially after the publication of Westcott and Hort's edition. There remain some proponents of the Byzantine text-type as the type of text most similar to the autographs. These include the editors of the Hodges and Farstad text and the Robinson and Pierpoint text.[1]

Translation of the King James Version
The Validity of Textus Receptus

In his book *Which Bible?* David Otis Fuller says this about Textus Receptus:

> Why did the early churches of the 2nd and 3rd centuries and all the Protestant Reformers of the 15th, 16th and 17th centuries choose Textus Receptus in preference to the Minority Text?
>
> The answer is because:
>
> Textus Receptus is based on the vast majority (90%) of the 5000+ Greek manuscripts in existence. That is why it is also called the Majority Text.

Textus Receptus is not mutilated with deletions, additions and amendments, as is the Minority Text.

Textus Receptus agrees with the earliest versions of the Bible: Peshitta (A.D. 150) Old Latin Vulgate (A.D. 157), the Italic Bible (A.D. 157) etc. These Bibles were produced some 200 years before the minority Egyptian codices favoured by the Roman Church. Remember this vital point.

Textus Receptus agrees with the vast majority of the 86,000+ citations from Scripture by the early church fathers.

Textus Receptus is untainted with Egyptian philosophy and unbelief.

Textus Receptus strongly upholds the fundamental doctrines of the Christian faith: the creation account in Genesis, the divinity of Jesus Christ, the virgin birth, the Saviour's miracles, his bodily resurrection, his literal return and the cleansing power of his blood!

Textus Receptus was—and still is—the enemy of the Roman Church. This is an important fact to bear in mind.[2]

Because of the above reasons, I believe the King James Version is an accurate translation from the original texts. In addition, my limited understanding of biblical Hebrew has demonstrated to me that the KJV translation gives us a full understanding of the original writings while not contradicting them. What I have seen is that, when read in context, the KJV does give us the correct meaning of the Scriptures. As we will see next, I do not have the same confidence with any of the newer English translations.

Chapter 21

"NEW AGE" INFLUENCE ON BIBLE TRANSLATIONS

As we look at the changes that have been made to the Bible and the fruit of those changes, I believe that there is no coincidence that these changes are strategic. We have to be mindful of the subtlety of the enemy. Satan first planted subtle deception in the minds of men and women, which then continued to spread through the ungodly philosophies they developed. This thinking then influenced the mindsets of other individuals, including some who eventually played important roles in Bible translation.

As we look at the subtle influence of the enemy, I first need to define a term.

What Is the "New Age"?

The encyclopedia defines the term *The New Age* (also known as the *New Age Movement, New Age spirituality,* and *Cosmic Humanism*) as a decentralized Western social and spiritual movement that seeks "Universal Truth" and the attainment of the highest individual human potential.[1] It includes aspects of astrology, esotericism, metaphysics, alternative medicine, music, collectivism, sustainability, and nature and pseudo-scientific interpretations of cosmology. New Age spirituality is characterized by an individual approach to spiritual practices and philosophies and the rejection of religious doctrine and dogma.

The New Age Movement includes elements of older spiritual and religious traditions, ranging from atheism and monotheism through classical pantheism, naturalistic pantheism, and panentheism to polytheism combined with science and Gaia philosophy.

New Age practices and philosophies sometimes draw inspiration from major world religions: Buddhism, Chinese folk religion, Christianity, Hinduism, Islam, Judaism, with particularly strong influences from East Asian religions, Gnosticism, Neopaganism, New Thought, Spiritualism, Theosophy, Universalism, and Western esotericism. Additional terms for the movement include *All is One* and *Mind-Body-Spirit*.

Some of the New Age Movement's constituent elements appeared initially in 19th-century metaphysical movements: Spiritualism, Theosophy, and New Thought; these movements in turn have roots in Transcendentalism, Mesmerism, and various earlier Western esoteric or occult traditions, such as the hermetic arts of astrology, magic, alchemy, and Kabbalah. The term *New Age* was used in this context in Madame H. P. Blavatsky's book *The Secret Doctrine*, published in 1888.

The Connection of the New Translations to the New Age

Elena Petrovna Gan (August 12, 1831-May 8, 1891), better known as Helena Blavatsky or Madame Blavatsky, born Helena von Hahn, was a founder of Theosophy and the Theosophical Society.

According to her own story as told to a later biographer, she spent the years 1848 to 1858 traveling the world, and is said to have visited Egypt, France, Canada (Quebec), England, South America, Germany, Mexico, India, Greece, and especially Tibet to study for two years with the men she called Brothers. She claimed to have become Buddhist while in Sri Lanka.

It was in 1873 that she immigrated to New York City. Impressing people with her professed psychic abilities, she was spurred on to continue her mediumship. Mediumship (among other psychical and spiritual sciences of the time), based upon the belief known as Spiritualism, which began at Rochester, New York, was a widely popular and fast-spreading field upon which Blavatsky based her career.

Throughout her career, she claimed to have demonstrated physical and mental psychic feats, which included levitation, clairvoyance, out-of-body projection, telepathy, and clairaudience. Another claim of hers was materialization, that is, producing physical objects out of nothing, though in general, her interests were more in the area of "theory" and "laws" rather than demonstration.

Foundation of Theosophical Society

Living in New York City, she helped found the Theosophical Society in September 1875, with Henry Steel Olcott, William Quan Judge, and others. Blavatsky wrote that all religions were both true in their inner teachings and problematic or imperfect in their external conventional manifestations. Her writings connecting esoteric spiritual knowledge with new science may be considered to be the first instance of what is now called New Age thinking, "the hippie movement of the last quarter of the nineteenth century."

H. P. Blavatsky was then forty-two years old and in controlled possession of her many and most unusual spiritual and occult powers. In the opinion of the Mahatmas, she was the best available instrument for the work they had in mind, namely to offer to the world a new presentation, though only in brief outline of the age-old *Theosophia*, "The accumulated Wisdom of the ages, tested and verified by generations of Seers...," that body of Truth of which religions, great and small, are but as branches of the parent tree. Her task was to challenge on the one hand the entrenched beliefs and dogmas of Christian Theology and on the other the equally dogmatic materialistic view of the science of her day. A crack, however, had recently appeared in the twofold set of mental fortifications. It was caused by Spiritualism, then sweeping America. To quote Helena's own words: "I was sent to prove the phenomena and their reality, and to show the fallacy of the spiritualistic theory of spirits."[2]

While on the surface the members of the third Reich looked like they had mostly political aims, they actually harbored many extreme and dangerous "religious" and mythological views, which in time they hoped to bring to the forefront of Germany. Hitler and his followers were fascinated by occultism and psychical research. One such fascination was with the teachings of a Madame Blavatsky, around the late 1800s early 1900s in a school of thought now called Theosophy. Theosophy was a conglomeration of teachings including occultism, research into ghosts and paranormal phenomena, and an extensive philosophical/religious base often based upon mythology, the gnostic new testament, a sort of "Atlantean cult," and "Alexandrian" teachings.

Quotes About Blavatsky

...Madame Blavatsky...stands out as the fountainhead of modern occult thought, and was either the originator and/or popularizer of many of the ideas and terms which have a century later been assembled within the New Age Movement. The Theosophical Society, which she cofounded, has been the major advocate of occult philosophy in the West and the single most important avenue of Eastern teaching to the West.[3]

Theosophy occupies a central place in the history of new spiritual movements, for the writings of Blavatsky and some of her followers have had a great influence outside of her organization....The importance of Theosophy in modern history should not be underestimated. Not only have the writings of

Blavatsky and others inspired several generations of occultists, but the movement had a remarkable role in the restoration to the colonial peoples of nineteenth century Asia their own spiritual heritage.[4]

Blavatsky's esoteric synthesis has served as a basic source for later esotericists, literati, scientists, and entire movements, including the New Age. Unlike most of her contemporaries, she is as visible today as any modern trendsetting guru, and she will most likely remain the most memorable and innovative esotericist of the 19th century.[5]

Followers of H.P. Blavatsky

Blavatsky's influence was widely felt, not only in certain philosophies adhered to by Hitler's Third Reich, but in the development of what is now referred to as "New Age" philosophies. Among Blavatsky's early circle of followers who met for study and séances were Arthur Conan Doyle, author of the Sherlock Holmes novels, and Westcott and Hort, who were Bible translators. Westcott and Hort and others of her followers helped found a society to study ghosts, which later became the "society for psychical research," which still exists, and studies many instances of paranormal phenomena.[6]

Who Were Westcott and Hort?

B.F. Westcott was born in 1825. F.J.A. Hort was born in 1828. They were members of the Broad Church (or High Church) Party of the Church of England. They became friends during their student days at Cambridge University. They worked for over 30 years together on the subject of the Greek text of the New Testament. Westcott went on to become the Bishop of Durham (England) and served for a while as chaplain to Queen Victoria. Hort is best remembered as a professor of divinity at Cambridge University. Both men wrote several books. They are best remembered for their edition of the Greek New Testament entitled, *The New Testament in the Original Greek*. They are also remembered for being the two most influential members of the English Revised Version committee, which produced a new English translation of the Bible. Frederick Henry Scrivener, an important text critic of the New Testament, thought that they exercised too much influence on this committee. Westcott died in 1901. Hort passed away in 1892. Both men had sons who collected their personal correspondence and who wrote biographies about them.[7]

The Doctrine of Westcott and Hort

It is clear that neither Westcott nor Hort held anything even faintly resembling a conservative view of Scripture. According to Hort's son, Hort's own mother (a devout Bible believer) could not be sympathetic to his views about the Bible. Westcott wrote to Hort that he overwhelmingly rejected the "idea of the infallibility of the Bible." Hort said the same thing, the same week, in a letter to Bishop Lightfoot. When Westcott became the Bishop of Durham, the Durham University Journal welcomed him with the praise that he was "free from all verbal or mechanical ideas of inspiration."[8]

Hort called the doctrine of the substitutionary atonement "immoral." In doing so, he sided with the normal doctrine of the High Church Party of the Church of England. The Low Church Party was generally evangelical, teaching salvation through personal faith in Jesus Christ. The High Church Party taught salvation by good works, including baptism and church membership. Westcott and Hort wrote many commentaries that include references to classic passages about salvation. Repeatedly their commentary is vague and unclear. Westcott taught that the idea of "propitiating God" was "foreign to the New Testament." He taught that salvation came from changing the character of the one who offended God. This is consistent with his statement that, "A Christian never is but is always becoming a Christian." Again and again, Westcott's vague comments about salvation are easy to interpret as teaching universal salvation.[9]

It was common in the days of Westcott and Hort for those in the Church of England who denied the deity of Christ to speak in vague terms! To clearly deny the deity of Christ was to jeopardize your position in the Church of England. Many High Church modernists learned to speak of the deity of Christ in unclear terms as a way to avoid trouble. Many statements by both Westcott and Hort fall into that category of "fuzzy" doctrinal statements about Christ. Westcott and Hort were brilliant scholars. Surely they were capable of expressing themselves clearly on the doctrine of Christ if they wanted to. At best they are unclear; at worst, they were modernists hiding behind the fundamental doctrinal statement of the Church of England.

Other Teachings of Westcott and Hort

There are many other areas that cause fundamental Bible believers to have serious questions about Westcott and Hort. Westcott denied that Genesis 1 through 3 were historically true. Hort praised Darwin and his theory of evolution. Both Westcott and Hort praised the "Christian socialist" movement of their day. Westcott belonged to several organizations designed to promote "Christian socialism" and served as president of one of them (the Christian Social Union).

Both Westcott and Hort showed sympathy for the movement to return the Church of England to Rome. Both honored rationalist philosophers of their time like Samuel Taylor Coleridge, Dr. Frederick Maurice, and Dr. Thomas Arnold. Both were serious students of the Greek philosophers Plato and Aristotle. There is much about the teaching of Westcott and Hort to deeply trouble any objective Bible believer.

Westcott and Hort's Influence on Translations

To put it bluntly, Westcott and Hort were very New Age in their thinking. They did not believe that the Bible was infallible or that humans are saved through faith in Jesus Christ. They were extremely liberal in their philosophy, and so they intended to retranslate the Bible to line up with their New Age philosophy. They were disciples of Helen Blavatsky, and they also agreed with the Alexandrian eastern belief in the occult, spirituality, and syncretism. Their dynamic equivalent translation of the New Testament reflected these beliefs.

The modern movement to revise the English Bible is based completely on the works of Westcott and Hort. Although most of the new versions that were influenced by Westcott and Hort use either formal equivalence or a combination of formal and dynamic equivalence, it is not as much the type of method used as the original manuscript that Westcott and Hort used as well as the doctrine that Westcott and Hort implemented through the corrupted text they used.

The following new Bible translations were influenced by Westcott and Hort and the New Age: New International Version (NIV), New American Standard Version (NASB), New King James Version (NKJV), New Revised Standard Version (NRSV), New American Bible (NAB), Revised English Bible (REB), Revised Standard Version (RSV), Contemporary English Version (CEV), Today's English Version (TEV), the Good News Bible, The Living Bible (TLB), Phillips, the New Jerusalem Bible, and the New Century Bible.

Here are what some scholars have to say about their work:

K.W. Clark wrote,

...the Westcott-Hort text has become today our Textus-Receptus. We have been freed from the one only to become captivated by the other...The psychological chains so recently broken from our fathers have again been forged upon us, even more strongly.[10]

E.C. Colwell wrote,

> The dead hand of Fenton John Anthony Hort lies heavy upon us.[11]

Zane Hodges, a long-time professor at Dallas Theological Seminary, wrote,

> Modern textual criticism is psychologically addicted to Westcott and Hort. Westcott and Hort in turn, were rationalists in their approach to the textual problem in the New Testament and employed techniques within which rationalism and every other kind of bias are free to operate.[12]

Alfred Martin, former Vice-President at Moody Bible Institute, wrote in 1951,

> The present generation of Bible students having been reared on Westcott and Hort have for the most part accepted this theory without independent or critical examination....if believing Bible students had the evidence of both sides put before them instead of one side only, there would not be so much blind following of Westcott and Hort.[13]

In the next chapter, we will address some of the evidence of how the New Age doctrine of Westcott and Hort has affected the new translations.

Chapter 22

SCRIPTURAL PROOFS OF THE "NEW AGE DOCTRINE"

I will admit that I am making many claims concerning the infiltration of dangerous doctrines into the Word of God. Many people have told me that this is irrelevant, that we really don't know what the Word of God really is. I disagree. As I said earlier, I do believe that God wants us to have the accurate Word of God. I also believe that in God's unlimited power and wisdom, He made a provision for us to have His inspired Word in the language that we currently speak. I also believe that it is in the devil's best interest to change the Word. To begin to question the authenticity of the Bible and its accuracy is a slippery slope that I believe is exactly what he wants us to venture down. I want to stress the point that the Bible as it was originally written is the God-breathed, inerrant Word of God. There have been many plots to subtly twist and distort the Bible to change the original intended messages. Through our historical journey from the original to the modern day, I look to point out the detours in the road and to correct them. To see where the enemy has looked to *"change times and laws"* (Dan. 7:25). To see the plans of the enemy is to correct the errors and to reconnect with the original intent of the Bible.

I want to make another thing clear: I have no stake in whatever Bible a person reads. I came across this information by simply wanting to know the truth. As mentioned in the Introduction, I found some major discrepancies between different translations, and I wanted to know why that was the case. I earnestly prayed and asked the Lord to allow me to know why there was such a big difference between Bible translations. The quest brought me to what you see here. It was about a four- to five-year journey, and what I found was really eye opening. As I said, the only reason I searched this out was to know the truth. I share this because I believe this is vitally important for the Body of Christ to know.

As Christians, our main priority has to be truth! God loves the truth because He is the truth; He is the source of absolute truth. To love truth means to love God. Truth should not gravitate around or be contingent upon our personal comfort or what we like or don't. Truth should be the driving force in our lives; it should be what we base our beliefs around. Once our realities and our perceptions clash with truth, then our realities and our perceptions must change. Our opinions should not attempt to change truth; truth should change our opinions.

So far we have seen how satan has been very strategic in seeking to change some very important doctrines of the Christian faith. I have laid out historical data showing the people who have been instrumental in achieving this goal. You can disagree with my opinion, but once you see the actual changes made in the Scriptures, I believe the evidence will be undeniable. The only question is: What is more important to you— truth or tradition and convenience? You must decide.

Let's look at some reasons why the new translations of the Word of God are dangerous to the Body of Christ and examine specific examples of how they have been changed.

One World Religion

We can see these new versions of the Bible as diluting the Word of God and becoming conducive to the "one world religion" that is talked about in the Book of Revelation.

By taking out the name of God or Jesus and substituting it with "the One," these versions allow the reader to substitute the God of their choice.

	KJV	NEW VERSIONS
John 1:14,18	"the only begotten of the Father" "the only begotten Son"	"the One and Only" "the One and Only"
Luke 9:35	"My beloved Son"	"My chosen One"
John 6:69	"Christ the Son of the living God"	"the Holy One"
John 4:42	"this indeed the Christ, the Saviour of the world"	"this One"

These versions also take away the words *he, his,* and *him,* which makes God and Jesus both men, in favor of a gender neutral word. "The One" of the new one world religion is neither male nor female. Some cults and other false religions worship the queen of heaven, as mentioned in the Book of Jeremiah (see Jer. 7:18; 44:17-19;25). The following verses in the newer versions all change the masculine pronouns *he, his,* or *him* to the gender neutral *the one:* John 7:18; John 9:37; John 12:45; John 15:21; Acts 7:38; Acts 10:21; Acts 22:9; First Corinthians 15:28; Colossians 3:10; Hebrews 5:7; Hebrews 7:21; First Peter 1:15; Revelation 2:1; Revelation 1:18. In Romans 1:20 and Acts 17:29, the word *Godhead* in the KJV is substituted with *divine nature.*

The newer translations also take away from the identity of the devil and even substitute references to Jesus and the true names of God.

Isaiah 14:12 in the KJV says, *"How art thou fallen from heaven, O Lucifer, son of the morning! how art thou cut down to the ground, which didst weaken the nations."* The NIV and the other new versions remove the name *lucifer* and substitute, *"O morning star, son of the dawn."* The problem with this is that morning star is one of the names that Jesus uses to refer to Himself:

> *I Jesus have sent Mine angel to testify unto you these things in the churches. I am the root and the offspring of David, and the bright and morning star* (Revelation 22:16).

Luke 4:8 in the KJV reads, *"And Jesus answered and said unto him, Get thee behind Me, Satan: for it is written, Thou shalt worship the Lord thy God, and Him only shalt thou serve."* The NIV and the NASB remove *"get thee behind me Satan."*

Holiness

The Bible tells us over and over again that holiness is an important part of being a true follower of God. First Peter 1:16 tells us to *"be ye holy; for I am holy"* (see also Lev. 19:2). The new versions remove the word *holy* in many places through the Scriptures. Without holiness, we are not in the image of God, and therefore, we have no power: *"Follow peace with all men, and holiness, without which no man shall see the Lord"* (Heb. 12:14).

In all of the following Scriptures, the word *holy*, found in the KJV, is removed in the NIV, NASB, and so forth:

> Second Peter 1:21—*"holy men"* in the KJV is replaced with just *"men"*

> Matthew 25:31—*"holy angels"* becomes just *"angels"*

First Thessalonians 5:27—*"holy brethren"* becomes *"brethren"*

Revelation 22:6—*"holy prophets"* becomes *"prophets"*

Revelation 18:20—*"holy apostles and prophets"* becomes *"apostles and prophets"*

In the following Scriptures, the *"Holy Ghost"* is replaced with just *"Spirit"*: Matthew 12:31; John 7:39; Acts 6:3; 8:18; First Corinthians 2:13.

Homosexuality

Apparently, the translators of the NIV and other new versions did not agree with the King James Version's assertion that homosexuality is wrong in the eyes of God. As a matter of fact, Virginia Mollenkott, one of the NIV translators, and Dr. Marten H. Woudstra, who was the chairman of the NIV Old Testament Committee and is now deceased, were reported to be openly homosexual.

> Dr. Woudstra, who died in the early 1990s, was a long-time friend of Evangelicals Concerned Inc. This organization was founded in 1976 by New York psychologist, Dr. Ralph Blair, as a nation-wide task force and fellowship for gay and lesbian "evangelical Christians" and their friends.
>
> Dr. Blair stated that Dr. Woudstra shared the viewpoint of ECI that lifelong "loving monogamous relationships" between gay men or women were acceptable to God. He believed that there was nothing in the Old Testament (his special area of technical expertise) that corresponded to "homosexual orientation". The "sodomy" of the OT simply involved temple rites and gang rape (Gen 19).
>
> "There is nothing in the Old Testament that corresponds to homosexuality as we understand it today." Dr. Virginia Mollenkott was quoted in the Episcopal Witness, June 1991, as stating, "My

lesbianism has always been a part of me." Her 1978 pro-homosexual book entitled *Is the Homosexual My Neighbor?* echoes her NIV assertion that the Bible censures only criminal offences like "prostitution and violent gang rape," not "sincere homosexuals... drawn to someone of the same sex."

Dr. Mollenkot details her pro-gay advocacy on her website: http://www.virginiarameymollenkott.blogs.com/. Her other books include *The Divine Feminine: Biblical Imagery of God as Female*; *Godding: Human Responsibility and the Bible*; and *Sensuous Spirituality: Out From Fundamentalism*.

Dr. Mollenkott served as stylistic consultant for the NIV and was a member of the National Council of Churches' Inclusive Language Lectionary Committee.[1]

The problem here is that because the above-mentioned authors disagreed with what we believe the Bible clearly states about homosexuality, they changed Scriptures to reflect what they believed. Again, as Christians, our lives must line up with God's Word, not the other way around!

In First Corinthians 6:9, the word *"effeminate"* in the KJV is changed to *"male prostitutes nor homosexual offenders."* In Deuteronomy 23:17; First Kings 15:12; 22:46; Second Kings 23:7, the word *"sodomites"* in the KJV is changed to *"shrine prostitutes."*

Fasting

The new versions try to take away some of the power that we as Christians receive from following the laws of God. We gain power through holiness, which includes forgiveness. We also gain power through fasting. Moses, Elijah, and even Jesus Christ Himself gained power from God by going through periods of fasting.

In the KJV, Matthew 17:21 says, *"Howbeit this kind goeth not out but by prayer and fasting."* This Scripture does not exist in the NIV.

Mark 9:29 in the KJV reads, *"And He said unto them, this kind can come forth by nothing, but by prayer and fasting."* In the NIV the word fasting is removed and the Scripture is written as such: *"He replied, 'This kind can come out only by prayer.'"*

Forgiveness

Mark 11:26 in the KJV is, *"But if ye do not forgive, neither will your Father which is in heaven forgive your trespasses."* This Scripture does not exist in the NIV.

In the KJV, Matthew 5:44 says, *"But I say unto you, Love your enemies, bless them that curse you, do good to them that hate you, and pray for them which despitefully use you, and persecute you."* The NIV only states in Matthew 5:44, *"But I tell you: Love your enemies and pray for those who persecute you."* I guess forgiveness was not that important to the NIV translators.

More Discrepancies Between the KJV and the NIV

Many words and phrases that are present in the King James Version were completely deleted from the New International Version. The NIV removes approximately 40 verses that are in the KJV. The NIV also deletes over 64,000 words, including words like *mercyseat, Jehovah,* and *Godhead.* It also removes meaningful, well-known Bible words like *Calvary, lucifer, New Testament, regeneration,* and so forth. Following are some examples:

Revelation 1:11 in the KJV reads: *"Saying, I am Alpha and Omega, the first and the last: and, What thou seest, write in a book, and send it unto the seven churches which are in Asia; unto Ephesus, and unto Smyrna, and unto Pergamos, and unto Thyatira, and unto Sardis, and unto Philadelphia, and unto Laodicea."* *"I am Alpha and Omega, the first and the last"* is removed in the new versions.

First John 5:7 in the KJV says, *"For there are three that bear record in heaven, the Father, the Word, and the Holy Ghost: and these three are one."* The new versions simply state, *"For there are three that testify,"* leaving out the mention of the Godhead.

In the KJV, Romans 11:6 says, *"And if by grace, then is it no more of works: otherwise grace is no more grace. But if it be of works, then it is no more grace: otherwise work is no more work." "But if it be of works, then it is no more grace"* is omitted from the new versions.

In the KJV, Acts 8:37 reads, *"And Philip said, If thou believest with all thine heart, thou mayest. And he answered and said, I believe that Jesus Christ is the Son of God."* This Scripture is completely removed from the NIV.

Other verses obscure the meaning or change it:

Philippians 4:13 in the KJV says, *"I can do all things through Christ which strengtheneth me."* The new versions omit the word *Christ* and substitute the word *Him.* Substitutions like this make the text less clear instead of more clear.

First Timothy 1:10 in the KJV says, *"For whoremongers, for them that defile themselves with mankind, for menstealers, for liars, for perjured persons, and if there be any other thing that is contrary to sound doctrine."* Of course, the words *"them that defile themselves with mankind,"* which is another way of saying "homosexuals," is removed from the NIV and changed to *"perverts."*

The Importance of Being Aware

These are just a few examples of the danger of following people who have tampered with the Word of God. It is clear to see that the new versions of the Bible were written with specific agendas. These new versions are not making the Word of God easier to understand; they are actually changing the meaning of the Holy Scriptures. We as humans do not have that authority. A very harsh judgment will fall on all those who tamper with the Word of God.

I need to take time out here to make a clarification. I mentioned some people who were instrumental to the translation of the NIV Bible. The reason it is so important to know what type of people they were is not to try to degrade or insult them. Knowing more about these translators and what they believe helps us see where they intentionally changed Scripture to fit their beliefs. We need to be aware of this. Once people start changing Scripture to suit their desires and wants, they have nullified the power in the Word of God. God is very adamant about the preservation of His Word. The Word is meant to change our thoughts and beliefs, not the other way around. We know the dangers that come from turning away from God's Word.

A Change of Heart

One Bible translator saw this danger for himself and had a change of heart. Franklin Logsdon (1907-1987) was a respected evangelical pastor and popular Bible conference speaker. He preached at Bible conferences (such as Moody Founder's Week) with well-known evangelists and pastors such as Billy Graham and Paul Smith of People's Church in Toronto.

In the 1950s, Logsdon was invited by his businessman friend, Franklin Dewey Lockman, to prepare a feasibility study that led to the production of the New American Standard Version of the Bible (NASV). He also helped interview some of the men who served as translators for this version. He wrote the Foreword that appears in the NASV.

As we see in the following testimony, in the later years of his life, Logsdon publicly renounced his association with the modern versions and stood unhesitatingly for the King James Bible. In a letter dated June 9, 1977, Logsdon wrote to Cecil Carter of Prince George, British Columbia:

> When questions began to reach me [pertaining to the NASV], at first I was quite offended. However, in attempting to

answer, I began to sense that something was not right about the NASV. Upon investigation, I wrote my very dear friend, Mr. Lockman, *explaining that I was forced to renounce all attachment to the NASV.* ...I can aver that the project was produced by thoroughly sincere men who had the best of intentions. The product, however, is grievous to my heart and helps to complicate matters in these already troublous times.[2]

So you can understand why the archenemy of God and humanity would want to do something to destroy this book. I ought to whisper to you, and this is no compliment to the devil, but he knows it can't be destroyed. He tried to destroy the Living Word. You don't see this depicted on Christmas cards, but the night Jesus Christ was born, the devil was there in that stable with one third of the fallen angels whom he had dragged down, to devour the manchild as soon as He was born (see Rev. 12:5). But he couldn't do it. Just think; satan was there when Jesus was born with all of those cohorts, those fallen angels, for one purpose: to devour the manchild. He couldn't do it. So failing to abort the Saviorhood of Jesus Christ, both at the manger and at the cross—when He said come down from the cross, inviting Jesus to come down before His work was finished—he is going to do what he knows is the next most effective thing. He is going to try to destroy the written Word.

There are places in this book where you can't differentiate between the living Word and the written Word. John 14:6 says, *"I am the life."* John 6:63 says, *"My words are life."* Different life? The same life. You can't differentiate because, after all, the written Word is the breath, if you please, of God, and Jesus Christ is God made flesh or the Word that came to Earth.

Chapter 23

MORE PROBLEMS WITH THE NEW TRANSLATIONS

THE DEITY OF CHRIST

Following are some examples of how the newer versions downplay the deity of Christ and the existence of His Kingdom.

> *And lead us not into temptation, but deliver us from evil: For Thine is the kingdom, and the power, and the glory, for ever. Amen* (Matthew 6:13 KJV).

> *And lead us not into temptation, but deliver us from the evil one* (NIV).

The NIV leaves out, *"For thine is the kingdom and the power and the glory for ever. Amen."* Everything pertaining to His Kingdom and deity is left out.

> *But seek ye first the kingdom of God, and His righteousness; and all these things shall be added unto you* (Matthew 6:33 KJV).

> *But seek first His kingdom and His righteousness, and all these things will be given to you as well* (NIV).

In the NIV, *"The kingdom of God"* is changed to *"His kingdom."*

And, behold, they cried out, saying, What have we to do with Thee, Jesus, Thou Son of God? art Thou come hither to torment us before the time? (Matthew 8:29 KJV)

"What do you want with us, Son of God?" they shouted. "Have You come here to torture us before the appointed time?" (NIV)

The NIV leaves out *"Jesus, Thou,"* degrading the power of the verse concerning His deity.

...While He spake these things unto them, behold , there came a certain ruler, and worshipped Him.... (Matthew 9:18 KJV).

While He was saying this, a ruler came and knelt before Him.... (NIV).

The NIV changes *"worshipped"* to *"knelt before."* People kneel before their own kings and queens, but they do not worship them. The NIV downplays the fact that Jesus is God and, therefore, is not worshipped. The KJV rightfully shows that Jesus was worshipped because He is God.

Jesus saith unto them, Have ye understood all these things? They say unto Him, Yea, Lord (Matthew 13:51 KJV).

"Have you understood all these things?" Jesus asked. "Yes," they replied (NIV).

The NIV leaves out *"Lord,"* again, leaving out His Lordship.

Then charged He His disciples that they should tell no man that He was Jesus the Christ (Matthew 16:20 KJV).

Then He warned His disciples not to tell anyone that He was the Christ (NIV).

The NIV leaves out *"Jesus,"* as it does in numerous other verses.

Then came to Him the mother of Zebedee's children with her sons, worshipping Him, and desiring a certain thing of Him (Matthew 20:20 KJV).

Then the mother of Zebedee's sons came to Jesus with her sons and, kneeling down, asked a favor of Him (NIV).

The NIV again changes "worshipping" to "kneeling down."

Watch therefore, for ye know neither the day nor the hour wherein the Son of man cometh (Matthew 25:13 KJV).

Therefore keep watch, because you do not know the day or the hour (NIV).

The NIV leaves out *"wherein the Son of man cometh."*

...Jesus came into Galilee, preaching the gospel of the kingdom of God (Mark 1:14 KJV).

... Jesus went into Galilee, proclaiming the good news of God (NIV).

The NIV says *"the good news"* and leaves out *"the gospel of the kingdom of God."*

But when he saw Jesus afar off, he ran and worshipped Him (Mark 5:6 KJV).

When he saw Jesus from a distance, he ran and fell on his knees in front of Him (NIV).

The NIV changes *"worshipped"* to *"fell on his knees."*

And straightway the father of the child cried out, and said with tears, Lord, I believe; help Thou mine unbelief (Mark 9:24 KJV).

Immediately the boy's father exclaimed, "I do believe; help me overcome my unbelief" (NIV).

The NIV leaves out the reference to Jesus as *"Lord."*

Blessed be the kingdom of our father David, that cometh in the name of the Lord: Hosanna in the highest (Mark 11:10 KJV).

Blessed is the coming kingdom of our father David! Hosanna in the highest (NIV).

The NIV changes His present Kingdom to a future one, saying, *"Blessed is the coming kingdom,"* and strips Jesus of His present Lordship.

Salvation by Faith and the Atonement

The newer versions also leave out some key verses and phrases regarding our salvation in Christ.

Matthew 9:13 in the KJV says, *"...For I am not come to call the righteous, but sinners to repentance."* The NIV says, *"...For I have not come to call the righteous, but sinners,"* leaving out *"to repentance."* So what are they called to?

"For the Son of man is come to save that which was lost," says Matthew 18:11 (KJV). The NIV leaves out the entire verse. This degrades His place as Savior, the purpose for which He came into the world.

When Jesus heard it, He saith unto them, They that are whole have no need of the physician, but they that are sick: I came not to call the righteous, but sinners to repentance (Mark 2:17 KJV).

On hearing this, Jesus said to them, "It is not the healthy who need a doctor, but the sick. I have not come to call the righteous, but sinners" (NIV).

The NIV leaves out *"to repentance,"* as it does in Matthew 9:13. Without this reference, we must ask, what is the sinner called to?

And the disciples were astonished at His words. But Jesus answereth again, and saith unto them, Children, how hard is it for them that trust in riches to enter into the kingdom of God (Mark 10:24 KJV).

This Scripture is replaced in the NIV with, *"The disciples were amazed at His words. But Jesus said again, "Children, how hard it is to enter the kingdom of God!"*

Some churches have amassed great riches and taught that men and women have to be prayed out of purgatory to get into Heaven, a primary means for these churches to get money from their believers. Many times giving money is used along with prayer in the Catholic Church as a means of getting sins forgiven. So leaving out *"for them that trust in riches"* allows them to use the verse to serve their own purposes.

And the Scripture was fulfilled, which saith, And He was numbered with the transgressors (Mark 15:28 KJV).

The NIV leaves out the entire verse.

But He turned and rebuked them, and said, Ye know not what manner of spirit ye are of (Luke 9:55 KJV).

But Jesus turned and rebuked them (NIV).

The NIV leaves out *"Ye know not what manner of spirit ye are of."*

For the Son of man is not come to destroy men's lives, but to save them. And they went to another village (Luke 9:56 KJV).

And they went to another village (NIV).

The NIV leaves out this entire section referring to Jesus as the Son of Man and Savior.

The change in the meaning of these two verses is unmistakable. They are not unintentional omissions or accidents. Look at the two verses together:

> *But He turned, and rebuked them, and said, Ye know not what manner of spirit ye are of. For the Son of man is not come to destroy men's lives, but to save them. And they went to another village* (Luke 9:55-56 KJV).

> *But Jesus turned and rebuked them, and they went to another village* (NIV).

> *Two men shall be in the field; the one shall be taken, and the other left* (Luke 17:36 KJV).

The NIV leaves out the entire verse.

> *For I am not ashamed of the gospel of Christ....* (Romans 1:16 KJV).

> *I am not ashamed of the gospel....* (NIV).

NIV leaves out *"of Christ."* So whose Gospel is it? What is the Gospel without Christ? And what power to save is there in a Gospel without Christ?

> *There is therefore now no condemnation to them which are in Christ Jesus, who walk not after the flesh, but after the Spirit* (Romans 8:1 KJV).

> *Therefore, there is now no condemnation for those who are in Christ Jesus* (NIV).

The NIV leaves out *"who walk not after the flesh, but after the Spirit."* It changes the entire meaning of the verse and leaves no requirement or prerequisite to being free from condemnation. In truth, the verse tells us that if we walk in the flesh, then there *is* condemnation for us. This has been taken out so that we won't know the truth.

> *...How beautiful are the feet of them that preach the gospel of peace, and bring glad tidings of good things* (Romans 10:15 KJV).

> *...How beautiful are the feet of those who bring good news* (NIV).

The NIV leaves out *"that preach the gospel of peace."* So what is the *"good news"* if it is not *"the gospel of peace"*? The Gospel of Jesus will bring peace to the one who puts his or her faith and trust in the finished works of Calvary and submits to His Lordship, for He is "the Prince of Peace" (see Isa. 9:6).

> *And if by grace, then is it no more of works: otherwise grace is no more grace. But if it be of works, then is it no more grace: otherwise work is no more work* (Romans 11:6 KJV).

> *And if by grace, then it is no longer by works; if it were, grace would no longer be grace* (NIV).

The NIV leaves out *"But if it be of works, then is it no more grace: otherwise work is no more work."* This section of Scripture is talking about the remnant according to the election of grace (verse 5) and the difference between grace and works. In verse five, the NIV leaves out *"election of grace."* Catholicism believes in salvation by works. The concept of grace through faith was what started the reformation—this was Martin Luther's key revelation.

And I am sure that, when I come unto you, I shall come in the fulness of the blessing of the gospel of Christ (Romans 15:29 KJV).

I know that when I come to you, I will come in the full measure of the blessing of Christ (NIV).

The NIV leaves out *"of the gospel."*

The blessings we receive come only because of Calvary and our faith in what Jesus accomplished for us on the Cross. The blessings of God only come to those who are obedient to the Gospel. All others are brought under God's judgment.

In flaming fire taking vengeance on them that know not God, and that obey not the gospel of our Lord Jesus Christ (2 Thessalonians 1:8 KJV).

He will punish those who do not know God and do not obey the gospel of our Lord Jesus (NIV).

For the time is come that judgment must begin at the house of God: and if it first begin at us, what shall the end be of them that obey not the gospel of God? (1 Peter 4:17 KJV)

For it is time for judgment to begin with the family of God; and if it begins with us, what will the outcome be for those who do not obey the gospel of God? (NIV)

What is Christ to us without the Gospel and His death, burial, and resurrection so that we may be redeemed from our sins?

For I delivered unto you first of all that which I also received, how that Christ died for our sins according to the Scriptures; And that He was buried, and that He rose again the third day according to the Scriptures (1 Corinthians 15:3-4 KJV).

For what I received I passed on to you as of first importance: that Christ died for our sins according to the Scriptures, that He was buried, that He was raised on the third day according to the Scriptures (NIV).

...Take, eat: this is My body, which is broken for you: this do in remembrance of Me (1 Corinthians 11:24 KJV).

...This is My body, which is for you; do this in remembrance of Me (NIV).

The NIV leaves out *"take eat"* and *"broken."* This is the core of communion, and its meaning is changed by the NIV. Catholics don't "break" the bread (representative of the body of the Lord Jesus), but eat what they say is the very body, soul, and blood of Christ transformed into the wafer.

And this I say, that the covenant, that was confirmed before of God in Christ, the law, which was four hundred and thirty years after, cannot disannul, that it should make the promise of none effect (Galatians 3:17 KJV).

What I mean is this: The law, introduced 430 years later, does not set aside the covenant previously established by God and thus do away with the promise (NIV).

The NIV leaves out *"in Christ."* There is no covenant without Christ. The New Testament or New Covenant is based on the shed blood of Jesus.

Wherefore thou art no more a servant, but a son; and if a son, then an heir of God through Christ (Galatians 4:7 KJV).

So you are no longer a slave, but a son; and since you are a son, God has made you also an heir (NIV).

The NIV leaves out the most significant and important part—
"*through Christ.*" We have no other means of salvation.

> *For in Christ Jesus, neither circumcision availeth any thing,
> nor uncircumcision, but a new creature* (Galatians 6:15 KJV).

> *Neither circumcision nor uncircumcision means anything;
> what counts is a new creation* (NIV).

The NIV leaves out *"for in Christ Jesus.*" Again, Christ is what
makes the difference. They keep leaving Him out!

> *For we are members of His body, of His flesh, and of His bones*
> (Ephesians 5:30 KJV).

> *For we are members of His body* (NIV).

The NIV leaves out *"of His flesh, and of His bones."*

> *In whom we have redemption through His blood, even the for-
> giveness of sins* (Colossians 1:14 KJV).

> *In whom we have redemption, the forgiveness of sins* (NIV).

The NIV leaves out *"through His blood."* What is the source or
means of our redemption? Where is the blood? Does not Hebrews 9:22
say, *"Without shedding of blood is no remission* [forgiveness]"? That verse
is in the NIV. Catholics do away with the finished works of Calvary
and crucify Him afresh, again and again. That's what the mass is all
about. They keep Jesus on the Cross; they serve a dead Jesus, not a risen
Savior. Roman Catholicism mirrors the New Age in regards to "salvation through works." Roman Catholic doctrine gives paths and actions
for one gaining eternal life. They put more trust in humanity than the
saving grace of God, which is received and not earned. Catholic repentance is tied to actions instead of grace. They also give ultimate power to

earthly priests and not the only acceptable mediator between God and humanity, which is Jesus.

The Second Coming of Christ

Watch therefore, for ye know neither the day nor the hour wherein the Son of man cometh (Matthew 25:13 KJV).

Therefore keep watch, because you do not know the day or the hour (NIV).

The NIV leaves out *"wherein the Son of man cometh,"* changing the whole meaning of the verse.

Deciding Which Version to Use

While many people will disqualify talk about bad and good translations, the overwhelming amount of contradictions between the newer versions and the authorized King James demonstrate that something is amiss. Unless God is schizophrenic, someone is wrong. Because of the translators' intent to change the meaning of the Scriptures and all these discrepancies, I believe the newer versions are dangerous. I believe that the King James Version should be used instead. As I said earlier, I am not trying to make the decision for you, just to let you know what I have discovered so you can choose wisely.

The authorized King James reflects a more conservative set of Christian doctrine, while the NIV and others reflect a very esoteric, New Age tone. The version was authorized by James VI & I (June 19, 1566–March 27, 1625), who was King of Scots as James VI from July 24, 1567. On March 24, 1603, he also became King of England and Ireland as James I when he inherited the English crown and thereby united the Crowns of the Kingdoms of Scotland and England.

The fact that the newer versions agree with other beliefs and Eastern religions is a clear indication that they have been watered down.

We have seen that the new translations include numerous Scriptures in which the name *Christ* has been taken out and *"the one"* has been added. We know that Eastern religions, such as Hinduism, worship many different gods, and the one-world syncretic religion has a very indistinct view of God. The God we serve is very specific, and His identity is in no means abstract. The god of syncretism is a god that has many paths. The God of Christianity only has one, and His name is Jesus. The Bible is very clear that we are peculiar to the ways of the world and that to be in agreement with the world is to be in opposition to Christ.

> *Ye adulterers and adulteresses, know ye not that the friendship of the world is enmity with God? whosoever therefore will be a friend of the world is the enemy of God* (James 4:4).

Jesus said in John 17:14, *"I have given them Thy word; and the world hath hated them, because they are not of the world, even as I am not of the world."*

How can the Body of Christ come into a unity of faith when we continue to use many different translations that have many different messages? Until we can agree on which English translation of the Bible to use, I do not believe that we will ever come together in unity of spirit. *"Can two walk together, except they be agreed?"* (Amos 3:3).

Ultimately, only revelation from the Holy Spirit can give us true understanding of the Scriptures. No level of human learning can really uncover the Word of God in its purest forms. There is power in the Word of God, and without that power, we as followers in Christ are like salt that has lost its savor. *"Forever, O LORD, Thy word is settled in heaven"* (Psalm 119:89).

Now that we have looked at some ways that satan has sought to change times and laws, in the final section we will look at how the power that was in the original Church can be ours today.

ELIJAH MUST
FIRST COME!

Chapter 24

THE SPIRIT AND POWER OF ELIJAH

SEEING THE SIGNS

We are in the last days—this is a statement that I can say without any fear of contradiction. The reason I can say this confidently is because the apostle Paul said it and that was around 2,000 years ago. If it was true then, it has to be even truer now. On a more specific note, when you see the signs of the times, it is clear that many of the prophetic signs are coming to pass. Israel is a nation. The world is moving to a one world economy and a one-world government. In the last few months, there have been earthquakes in many different (divers) places (see Matt. 24:7). There was even an earthquake recently in Camp Hill, Pennsylvania, a place that very seldom has earthquakes. When you add these signs with the earthquakes in Chile, Haiti, and Japan, and the large volcanic activity in Iceland, it seems clear that Jesus is soon to return.

The Bible says that these signs will happen before the end comes. Jesus referred to an old Jewish saying about the fact that one sign alone does not mean a lot, but when a bunch of signs occur together, something is up (see Luke 17:37). To paraphrase: If you see one vulture, it is no big deal. But when you see a group of vultures circling around, then you know that there is a dead body around.

We have always seen earthquakes; we have always had wars and rumors of wars. The frequency of the signs is what is a clear indication that something big is going to happen. The Bible says that all creation groans in expectation for the sons and daughters of God to be revealed (see Rom. 8:19-22). We are seeing those groanings now as the Messiah is soon to return.

We as the Church must come to the realization that Jesus won't just return on a whim. He will return in response to His Bride bidding Him to come (see Rev. 22:17). He is coming back for a spotless Bride who is devoid of the blemishes of the world. Jesus did all that He had to do on the Cross; He is waiting for us to walk in the fullness of what He has called us to.

That being said, what is it that is left for us as Christ's Bride to do? I have outlined two of the major things that have drawn us away from God. The enemy has changed God's appointed times for most Christians. He has also attempted to separate us from following the inspired Word of God. As these two elements are restored, we will walk in a greater level of intimacy with Jesus. This intimacy is what will return us to the power that was known in the first Church.

This final section is about the spirit that the Lord is releasing in order to make this happen. That spirit is the spirit and power of Elijah!

Elijah Will Come

> And His disciples asked Him, saying, why then say the scribes that Elias must first come? And Jesus answered and said unto them, **Elias truly shall first come, and restore all things.** But I say unto you, That Elias is come already, and they knew him not, but have done unto him whatsoever they listed. Likewise shall also the Son of man suffer of them. **Then the disciples understood that He spake unto them of John the Baptist** (Matthew 17:10-13).

Jesus is speaking in three tenses here. We know that Elijah had actually already come. We know the Old Testament prophet Elijah the Tishbite had come to correct Israel many centuries before. We also see Jesus referring to John the Baptist as Elijah; John was not literally Elijah, but Jesus is speaking of the spirit in which Elijah walked. The last tense is a future tense. *"Elijah truly shall come"* is a promise that Elijah will return in the future. This will happen before the second coming of the Messiah.

Jesus is quoting from the Old Testament:

> *The LORD is well pleased for His righteousness' sake; He will magnify the law, and make it honourable. But this is a people robbed and spoiled; they are all of them snared in holes, and they are hid in prison houses: they are for a prey, and none delivereth; for a spoil, and none saith,* **Restore** *(Isaiah 42:21-22).*

In this passage of Scripture, the Lord is prophetically telling us what will happen in the future return of Elijah. The Lord will come to open the blind eyes and to set the captives free.

> *Behold My servant, whom I uphold; Mine elect, in whom My soul delighteth; I have put My spirit upon Him: He shall bring forth judgment to the Gentiles. He shall not cry, nor lift up, nor cause His voice to be heard in the street. A bruised reed shall He not break, and the smoking flax shall He not quench: He shall bring forth judgment unto truth. He shall not fail nor be discouraged, till He have set judgment in the earth: and the isles shall wait for his law. Thus saith God the LORD, He that created the heavens, and stretched them out; He that spread forth the earth, and that which cometh out of it; He that giveth breath unto the people upon it, and spirit to them that walk therein: I the LORD have called thee in righteousness, and will*

hold thine hand, and will keep thee, and give thee for a cov-
enant of the people, for a light of the Gentiles; **To open the**
blind eyes, to bring out the prisoners from the prison,
and them that sit in darkness out of the prison house. *I*
am the LORD: *that is My name: and My glory will I not give*
to another, neither My praise to graven images. Behold, the
former things are come to pass, and new things do I declare:
before they spring forth I tell you of them (Isaiah 42:1-9).

Restoring the Torah

The Lord will magnify the Torah and make it honorable. The
people are in bondage and are being robbed because they have not kept
the Torah! The spirit of Elijah does not turn us away from the Torah; it
turns us back to following the Torah. Following the Torah frees us and
removes us from bondage. Jesus came to set the captives free by empow-
ering them to follow the Torah.

> **Restore:** שׁוּב shûb (pronounced shoob) A primitive root; to
> turn back; generally to retreat; often adverbially "again."[1]

Generally speaking, Isaiah shows us that Elijah will come and will
proclaim restoration to God's people, restoration to God's Word. Notice
when Jesus mentions John the Baptist He reiterates that John will tell us
to restore the teaching of the Torah. John preached a message of repentance. *Repentance* simply means to turn back to the truth. The prefix *re*
means again or to turn back, and the root word for *pent* is where we get
the word *truth*.

Bondage vs. Power

As we saw in Chapter 8, one of the greatest misunderstandings in the
Church today is the term *bondage* or *legalism*. Whenever people begin
to teach on returning to the teachings of the Torah, they are accused of
trying to place believers in bondage. They have also been described as

being "legalistic." Many even quote passages from Galatians and Colossians as the proof that we are not to return back to the bondage of the Law. This is an example of taking Scripture out of context. We have already discussed that in his letter to the Galatians, Paul was writing to former pagans, telling them not to go back into their pagan practices. Paul was not writing to Jews who were following the Torah.

The Bible actually says just the opposite of bondage: The Bible shows us that by walking in the Torah we find true liberty. It is when we don't walk in the laws of God that we find ourselves in bondage. *"So shall I keep Thy law continually for ever and ever. And I will walk at liberty: for I seek Thy precepts"* (Ps. 119:44-45).

Think about true bondage. Have you ever seen people caught in drug addictions that they can't overcome? Have you ever been around people who have problems with pornography or sex addiction? What about women in abusive relationships who just can't seem to leave their abusers? The devil and sin are what put us in bondage. God doesn't want to put us in bondage. All His laws and commandments are to bless us and prosper us. His plans are to give us success and to bring us into closer relationship with Him. The devil wants us in bondage to him, which brings death and destruction. He knows that if he can separate us from following God's Word, then we are open targets because we have no power.

God wants us to overcome the lies and the deceits of the enemy that are meant to destroy us. He wants to open our eyes to the fact that we have placed ourselves in bondage by not keeping His laws. We desperately need to restore the Body of Christ to the teaching and the training of the Holy Scriptures!

Lining Our Minds Up With His Word

Elijah's primary message is to turn the people back to the Torah. Elijah wants to empower God's people to walk in the anointing that God intended for them to walk into.

For, behold, the day cometh, that shall burn as an oven; and all the proud, yea, and all that do wickedly, shall be stubble: and the day that cometh shall burn them up, saith the LORD of hosts, that it shall leave them neither root nor branch. But unto you that fear My name shall the Sun of righteousness arise with healing in His wings; and ye shall go forth, and grow up as calves of the stall. And ye shall tread down the wicked; for they shall be ashes under the soles of your feet in the day that I shall do this, saith the LORD of hosts. **Remember ye the law of Moses My servant, which I commanded unto him in Horeb for all Israel, with the statutes and judgments. Behold, I will send you Elijah the prophet before the coming of the great and dreadful day of the LORD: And he shall turn the heart of the fathers to the children, and the heart of the children to their fathers, lest I come and smite the earth with a curse** (Malachi 4:1-6).

The first thing that God needs to do with us is to get our minds lined up with His Word. *Repent* actually means to turn our minds back to the truth. Once our minds are lined up with God's, then we can walk in agreement with Him. God's Word represents His mind. The Torah reveals the heart of God to us. Out of the overflow of the heart the mouth speaks (see Luke 6:45). The Bible represents the Word of God. Therefore, we can conclude that God spoke the Torah out of the overflow of His heart.

This is an important element in getting closer to God. Once we understand how God thinks and acts, then we can walk closer in agreement with Him. This is what the Law of God is all about. God has better things to do than to give us a bunch of arbitrary laws. Because He desires that we succeed and are successful in life, He is diligent to compel us to follow His Word. As stated earlier, God is a God of purpose. Not one of

God's laws or commandments is without significance. That is why Jesus refers to every *"jot and tittle"* remaining in Matthew 5:18. All of God's laws are important. Every word of God has a meaning behind it. Even if we think it is unimportant and can't see the purpose to it, there is a real meaning behind every word that proceeds out of the mouth of God.

Chapter 25

THE PEACE OF GOD

Peace is a concept that we need to understand better in order to understand Jesus. Jesus is the Prince of Peace, and since He is in charge of peace, then we have to know what His peace is. The Hebrew word for *peace* is *shalom*. In Jewish culture, a person wishes shalom for others when meeting them or when leaving them. It is an all-encompassing word.

Not Like the World's Peace

> ***Peace** I leave with you, My **peace** I give unto you: not as the world giveth, give I unto you. Let not your heart be troubled, neither let it be afraid* (John 14:27)

Jesus says He gives us peace that is different from the world's peace. In the world we think of peace as an abstract state of being that basically means the absence of stress or strife. If I yell out in my house that I want "peace and quiet," I would assume that my children would sit still and no one would call me or talk to me. That is the world's concept of peace. God's concept of peace is different. Peace to God is an actual thing, not a state of being. We will get to that shortly, but for now, keep that in mind.

These things I have spoken unto you, that in Me ye might have **peace**. *In the world ye shall have tribulation: but be of good cheer; I have overcome the world* (John 16:33).

Jesus says here that He has given us His Word so that we can have peace. He then goes on to let us know that He has overcome the world. Jesus' Word helps us overcome the world by giving us His peace. In order to understand this more, we will look closer of God's peace and how it applies to us.

For I know the thoughts that I think toward you, saith the LORD, *thoughts of* **peace**, *and not of evil, to give you an expected end* (Jeremiah 29:11).

God's thoughts are for us to have an expected end; God's expected end is for us to have prosperity and to be successful in life. Our prosperity and our success come through God's peace. So how do we get all these things through God's peace?

Peace (NT) εἰρήνη eirēnē i-rah'-nay probably from a primary verb εἴρω eirō (to *join*); *peace* (literally or figuratively); by implication *prosperity:*—one, peace, quietness, rest, + set at one again.

Peace שלום shâlôm (shaw-lome') *safe,* that is, (figuratively) *well, happy, friendly*; also (abstractly) *welfare,* that is, health, **prosperity.** Ancient Hebrew is said to have developed from a picture form of words.[1]

The ancient word picture of shalom spells out the concept of destroying (shin) the authority that establishes chaos. God establishes His order that destroys the authority that establishes chaos.

ש- To destroy

ל- The authority

ו- that establishes

ם- chaos

Chaos is of the *devil*. Peace is of the Lord!

The Order of God's Kingdom

As we see here, God's peace represents His authority, which destroys and replaces the chaos that comes from the world. The peace of God represents His order, which allows us to be blessed, to prosper, and to have the order to replace the chaos that comes from the world. Since God is not the author of confusion, it is safe to assume that the devil is.

In Genesis 1, the Bible tells us that the Earth was without form and void. God then spoke and brought order to the chaos that was in the world. God's Word gives us His peace by giving us the order of the Kingdom of God. God's peace brings us prosperity and completeness. Jesus came and re-implemented the order of the Kingdom of God. He overcame the world by His Word and by walking in the Torah. We, on the other hand, have His shalom.

The peace of God is the order of the Kingdom of God, which is His Law. By following the Law of God, we receive the Lord's blessing and His prosperity that He meant for us. Because His peace is all-encompassing, it is relevant to every aspect of our lives. It is not just limited to the concept of not sinning. God has given us much more than just the moral law. He gives us laws that put our entire life in order and bring us success in every way—His way. We miss out on God's completeness for our lives when we turn away from His order and, therefore, reject His peace.

God's ultimate goal is to bring the Kingdom authority of God to the Earth. Adam originally had the authority of the Kingdom of God when he was told to multiply and to take dominion of the Earth. Adam was made in the image of God; he thought and acted like God. Once Adam turned away from God by his disobedience to God's Word, he began agreeing with satan instead. From that point on, God has looked to re-implement the authority of His Kingdom through His people. That is why the Bible refers to Jesus as the *"last Adam"* (see 1 Cor. 15:45). That is why Jesus told us to pray *"on earth as it is in Heaven"* (see Matt. 6:10). Jesus was teaching us to agree with the authority of God's Kingdom and, therefore, usher in the Kingdom's agenda in the Earth. God's Word is established in Heaven, and our job is to establish His Word and authority here on the Earth.

> *For there are three that bear record in heaven, the Father, the Word, and the Holy Ghost: and these three are one* (1 John 5:7).

God is looking for His people to bear record on the Earth by agreeing with His Word and to re-establish His Kingdom authority on the Earth. That is what the ministry of Elijah is all about: turning God's people back to (restore) God's authority by urging them back to the original and absolute truth of God's Word.

Chapter 26

KEEPING THE TORAH

WHAT IS THE TORAH?

We have used the word *Torah* several times in this book, so it is only proper that we seek a deeper understanding of what the Torah is. The Church traditionally has described the Torah as the Law of God. The English translations of the Bible actually use the word *law* instead of *Torah*. Primarily because of the anti-Semitic tone that is prevalent in Christianity, we have defined the Torah as something that is negative. The *Law* is a word that sounds burdensome and oppressive, therefore making it easier to turn away from. We have missed out on many of God's blessings by turning away from the Torah.

The Torah is traditionally known as the first five books of the Bible, the books that God dictated through Moses to Israel in the wilderness. The Torah includes the Books of Genesis, Exodus, Leviticus, Numbers, and Deuteronomy. It has been translated in English as the Law, while in reality the Torah is the teaching and instruction of God. It is the blueprint that God has given His people to help them live prosperously on this side of glory.

*This **book** of the **law** shall not depart out of thy mouth; but thou shalt meditate therein day and night, that thou mayest observe*

to do according to all that is written therein: for then thou shalt
make thy way prosperous, and then thou shalt have good success
(Joshua 1:8).

Here in the Book of Joshua we have the Lord giving a commandment to Joshua to give to the people. Moses had just died and left Joshua
in charge. God is repeating the commandment that He had given
through Moses for the Israelites to keep the Torah so that they would
be successful.

In the book before Joshua, the Book of Deuteronomy, God had just
finished giving the Torah, and He urged His people to make a choice.
He set before His people life and death, blessing and cursing. He then
told them to choose life so that they and their seed would live. God says
that the Torah is the word of life, and we will have a prosperous life
when we follow it. God also equates following the Torah with having
love for Him: *"If you love Me you will keep My commandments."* Jesus
also repeats this commandment (see John 14:15).

Results of Following the Torah

God was urging His people to keep the Torah as a demonstration of
their love for Him. By keeping the Torah, we are successful in every aspect
of our lives. God loves us and wants us to be successful. Like any good
parent, God gets joy through the success of His children. We also glorify
God by our godly success, which should provoke others to want to know
all about the God whom we serve. We become living testimonies to God
when we allow the Word of God to work in our lives. When the world
sees God's people prospering while walking in the Torah, they have no
other recourse but to acknowledge that God is real and that His Word is
true. People often like to argue opinions, but results cannot be disputed.

Another result that comes from walking in Torah is victory over our
enemies. God promised Joshua that when the Israelites walked in Torah
no one would be able to stand against them. None of their enemies could

defeat Israel when they truly walked in Torah—now that is power! As a matter of fact, when Joshua and the children of Israel lost a battle, they knew something was wrong, that this was not meant to be. Israel believed that they were the head and not the tail because that is what God said about them. Whenever they were overcome by their enemies, it was a result of turning away from God.

> *And the LORD said unto Joshua, Get thee up; wherefore liest thou thus upon thy face? Israel hath sinned, and they have also transgressed My covenant which I commanded them: for they have even taken of the accursed thing, and have also stolen, and dissembled also, and they have put it even among their own stuff. Therefore the children of Israel could not stand before their enemies, but turned their backs before their enemies, because they were accursed: neither will I be with you any more, except ye destroy the accursed from among you* (Joshua 7:10-12).

God truly operates in types and shadows. He used Israel in the Old Testament as a type in the natural of what the Church in the New Testament experiences spiritually. Repentance was Israel's only hope. Whenever we turn away from His Word, we lose the battles against our enemies. When we walk in agreement to the Word of God, there is nothing that we cannot overcome.

Think again about Mount Sinai and the first covenant. God told the people of Israel that by keeping His commandments they would be a special group of people who would be better than those around them. Historically, Israel developed a reputation in ancient times because their culture was so different from the nations around them.

> *Now therefore, if ye will obey My voice indeed, and keep My covenant, then **ye shall be a peculiar treasure unto Me above all people**: for all the earth is Mine* (Exodus 19:5).

They were healthier and wealthier than all the other nations of the world. This represents the time that Israel was in the desert. God tells them that they did not get sick and even their clothes did not wear out for the 40 years they were in the desert. The other proof that the Word of the Lord is true is that the Orthodox community has remained intact through over 4,000 years of persecution and atrocities. Judaism has survived even when most of the other nations around them were destroyed. When was the last time you saw a Philistine? This is not a coincidence, but proof that God's Word is true!

Additional Meanings of Torah

> Law- הרות הרת tôrah torah *to-raw', to-raw'* a *precept* or *statute*, especially the *Decalogue* or *Pentateuch:*—law.

> The Torah also means- הרי ארי yarah yara' (*yaw-raw'*), A primitive root; properly to *flow* as water (that is, to *rain*); transitively to *lay* or *throw* (especially an arrow, that is, to *shoot*); figuratively to *point* out (as if by *aiming* the finger), to *teach:*— (+) archer, cast, direct, inform, instruct, lay, shew, shoot, teach (-er, -ing), through.—to hit the mark.[1]

The Hebrew word picture for the word *Torah* is to hit the mark. The word *sin*, on the other hand, means to miss the mark. I like to describe following the Word of God in terms of getting closer to God. God is the source of life because He is the Creator of life. The more our lives agree with God, the more we have life. That is why Jesus tells us He came to give us life more abundantly (see John 10:10). He is life itself because He created it.

If you think in terms of death not being a thing in itself, then death is the absence of life. In the same manner, darkness is not an entity; it is the absence of light. Jesus is also the Creator and source of light. The Torah is a *"lamp unto my feet, and a light unto my path"* (Ps. 119:105).

We just saw that sin is to miss the mark or to turn away from God. God and His Word are one. Therefore, to walk away from Him is to not follow His Word; they are one and the same.

When Paul writes that the wages of sin is death, he is stating the fact that when we sin and turn away from God's Word, death is an automatic result. God is not punishing us; we are willingly entering into death by rebelling against His Word. That is why God urged Israel to *"...choose life, that both thou and thy seed may live"* (Deut. 30:19).

When God told Adam that if he disobeyed His Word he would surely die, He was trying to save Adam from living without being connected to the source of life. Adam died spiritually because He separated himself from the source of life, the living Word of God.

Inward Peace and Outward Success

Prosperous- צלח tsaleach, *(tsaw-lay'-akh)*A primitive root; to *push* forward, in various senses (literally or figuratively, transitively or intransitively).[2]

When we follow the Torah, prosperity is literally forced upon us. The psalmist tells us that goodness and mercy shall follow us all the days of our lives when we dwell in the house (the presence) of the Lord (see Ps. 23:6).

And it shall come to pass, if thou shalt hearken diligently unto the voice of the LORD thy God, to observe and to do all His commandments which I command thee this day, that the LORD thy God will set thee on high above all nations of the earth: And all these blessings shall come on thee, and overtake thee, if thou shalt hearken unto the voice of the LORD thy God (Deuteronomy 28:1-2).

Success is defined as *"outcome, result, degree, or measure of succeeding."* God doesn't just want us to have peace on the inside. He promises that when we follow His Word, we will have a measured outcome of success in our lives. That is what He wants to use to bring others into the saving knowledge of Him. When we succeed in life by the power of God, it brings Him glory and acts as a witness to others that God is faithful and true.

> *All scripture is given by inspiration of God, and is profitable for doctrine, for reproof, for correction, for instruction in righteousness* (2 Timothy 3:16).

I always like to remind everyone that all the references in the Bible to "the Scriptures" are talking about the Old Testament. There was no New Testament during the time when Jesus and the apostle Paul were walking around ministering. If we believe that all Scripture is truly *"God breathed"* and is for our benefit, then why would we not want to follow it? We cannot fully trust God if we don't have faith in His Word. If we feel as though our plans may work out for us outside of God's Word, then we must think that we know as much as God does. All Scripture is given for our benefit, and it is in our best interest to follow it because it prepares us for God's work. All Scripture means *all.*

As mentioned earlier, I am not a Hebrew scholar. I do have a slight knowledge of biblical Hebrew; it is elementary at best. I am still studying and learning the deeper complexities of the Torah and the Word of God. I have not memorized all 613 laws of the Torah, nor do I claim to be able to completely follow all of them. I do claim that the Torah is the Word of God and that it brings life and prosperity to those who follow it. Blessings come from following God's laws, and my job is to urge the Body of Christ to enter into a deeper relationship with the Messiah through studying and walking in the way of the Lord. We are stronger when we follow the Bible, and we will be defeated when we don't.

Three Categories of Torah

The Torah is broken into three primary categories: 1) the moral laws, 2) ceremonial laws, and 3) civil laws. All of these laws help the believer to have God's peace and receive the prosperity that God has intended for His people. As a matter of fact, God's laws work for people whether or not they acknowledge God. God is the Creator, and the process that He used to give us His Word is the same process that He used to create the universe. God's Spirit was present, God spoke, and it was done. It is like gravity. Gravity is a law that was created by God. Even those who do not acknowledge God are still affected by gravity. I could disbelieve that gravity exists all I want, but it will not change the fact that if I jump off the roof of my house, I will hit the ground or whatever happens to be underneath me.

The spiritual laws of God are actually more real than the natural laws. As a matter of fact, since everything that we see originates from the spirit realm, the spiritual laws are more real than the natural laws. Just because we don't immediately see the results of breaking God's spiritual laws, it does not negate the fact that they are real. Our faith is what convinces us that when we follow the laws of God we do get the results that God said that we will get.

Faith is one of the greatest battles going on in the U.S. This country has been blessed more than any other nation because we have acknowledged the laws of God. Our constitution and our civil laws reflect the Judeo-Christian form of law. I don't have the time to go into great detail on this, but the founding fathers made mention of the God of the Bible in the original documents of the forming of the United States of America.

The civil and moral laws of God are meant to bring peace and order to civilization. When they are used to govern a nation, that nation prospers. When we turn away from God and break His laws, we are doomed for failure. As with individuals, following the path of God brings blessings, and rebellion brings curses upon a nation.

There are three types of laws in the Torah, moral, ceremonial, and cultural laws. The moral laws of God are the ones that let us know what is right and what is wrong. The Ten Commandments fall into the category of moral laws. The ceremonial laws were laws that determined the way that animal sacrifices were carried out. Although we do not have to sacrifice animals, Paul tells us that the ceremonies (or feasts) of the Lord teach us about the nature and the plan of God. Jesus fulfilled the sacrifices, so we no longer need to kill animals for atoning of our sins. The cultural laws teach us a lot about how to live with other people and other cultures. Although all laws teach us about God and have great benefit to us, we must also use wisdom in following the ceremonial and cultural laws of the Torah.

Chapter 27

MY STORY AND THE TORAH

Following God's laws is not just a pleasant idea for me; my life is proof that it works. It would be one thing if I just encouraged others to walk in Torah. I believe in God's Word with all my heart because I have seen the dramatic things that following Torah has done in my life. As I have said, it is one thing to debate opinions, but you cannot argue with the facts.

Many people have heard my testimony of how I turned away from God and how I found myself divorced, homeless, and addicted to drugs. (You can read my entire testimony in my book *From Kilos to the Kingdom*.) I knew that I was outside of God's plan for my life and that I had to repent and start living for God. Like many people, I was not sure exactly how I was supposed to live for God. I knew the basics, but my Christian upbringing had more Baptist tradition than pure biblical teaching.

I began to really search the Scriptures to find the answers to my life. There were so many things that I needed to change. I didn't know where to start. Then one day I came across the Scripture in Joshua 1:8, which spoke to me. I realized that the more of the Word I ingested into my spirit, the better my chances for success in life were. I also knew that it was not enough to just read the Word and know it, but I had to also walk in the Word as much as I could.

I am now happily married, and I no longer use drugs. I own two radio stations and am the head pastor of a church that my wife and I founded in January 2010. I have traveled the world preaching the Gospel, and I am a published author. I do not brag on myself, but only that I was smart enough to realize that the Word of God works. God is faithful and true, and He will do exactly what He has promised if you believe.

Keys for Health

Now I want to give a specific example of how the Torah blesses us in every detail of life. My family on my dad's side has a history of high blood pressure. Most of the men in the family died relatively early due to blood diseases. Whether it was through stroke, heart attack, or any other blood-related disease, they died early. My father is still alive at 70 years of age, but he takes a large amount of medication. The last I checked, I believe he takes over 20 pills a day. I want to avoid that type of lifestyle.

The Bible says that God will visit the iniquities of the fathers through three or four generations (see Exod. 20:5). Generational curses can come from not following the Torah. These curses are not simply God punishing people, but as I stated earlier, they are an automatic result of not following God's Word. Blessings come from walking in agreement with God while curses come from not obeying the Torah.

Many cases of high blood pressure, cancer, and diabetes are generational curses. That is why medical surveys ask you about your family history. When you are pre-disposed for certain diseases based on family history, it is because something has been passed down through your family bloodline. Think about what God says in Exodus 15:26 and Deuteronomy 7: 9-16

*And said, If thou wilt diligently hearken to the voice of the
LORD thy God, and wilt do that which is right in His sight,
and wilt give ear to His commandments, and keep all His statutes, I will put none of these diseases upon thee, which I have
brought upon the Egyptians: for I am the LORD that healeth
thee* (Exodus 15:26).

Here God equates keeping His commandments with not getting
diseases and with being physically healed. If that is the case, then we
also have to believe that the opposite is true: By not following the commandments of God, we *will* get the diseases that the other nations get.

My blood pressure was higher than normal all of my life. I remember getting a physical to play basketball when I was 15 years old. At that
time, the doctor told me that he would need to see me in 20 years. His
diagnosis was based on my race and the fact that at 15 years old, my
blood pressure was higher than it should have been. I was not over-
weight, and I was in very good physical condition because I ran and
played sports constantly. But at 15 years old, I was already showing signs
of having a problem with my blood pressure. This same pattern followed
me throughout my adult life, through college, and through the military.
Even though I was in excellent physical condition, there was a problem.

While reading the Bible, I came across a list of foods that God said
not to eat. I fasted and prayed and went into an intense time of study,
seeking the deep and profound meaning behind these declarations of
God. I want the entire world to know the secret things of God. The
truth that the Holy Spirit spoke to me that was so overpowering during
my intense time of seeking answers was this—*because they are not good
for you!* God forbid His people from eating certain animals because they
were not intended for food. He created pigs and other scavengers to
clean up the diseases and germs from humans. Because God wants us to
be healthy, He outlined certain dietary laws to help us be healthy.

When ships are in the middle of the ocean, they dispel their trash and waste into the ocean. It is the job of the scavengers to clean up the trash and the waste from the middle of the ocean. Lobsters, shrimp, and so forth clean up bacteria from the ocean. That is why a vulture can eat a dead body and not get sick. A pig can get bitten by a poisonous snake and not die. Their flesh is made to absorb poison and diseases. God tried to protect us from these things by giving us the scavengers and then warning us not to eat them. Humans, in our foolishness, go and eat them anyway.

Laws for a Better Life

A lack of understanding has taught us that these laws are no longer valid. Following God's dietary laws will not get you into Heaven, but they are meant to give you a better life. God cares about your physical welfare almost as much as your eternal soul. That is the reason that He gave us His laws—so that we can prosper and be in good health even as our souls prosper (see 3 John 2). We demonstrate our faith by following God's Word, but we bring Him glory when that obedience pays off through having a successful life. The Gospels are for your eternal soul, but the laws are to give you success in this world!

To finish my testimony, I am now in my 40s, and my blood pressure is habitually in the 120 over 80 range—normal. It is no coincidence, simply proof that God's Word works for our benefit.

African Americans tend to consume a large amount of pork and other scavengers. We also have a higher rate of hypertension and certain forms of cancer than most other ethnic groups in this nation. This is not a coincidence. Originally this was imposed on the African American culture during the time of slavery because we had to eat whatever we were given on the plantations. We have adopted that culture and it has caused a disproportionate amount of sickness and death in the community.

Think about how deceived we Christians have been for so long. We brag about the fact that we can eat whatever we want to and that we are no longer "under the Law." We need to realize that it is obedience to the Word of God that brings us life and brings it to us more abundantly. God is God regardless of our actions; we are the ones who become better through obedience to the Torah.

Chapter 28

CHRIST HAS NO POWER UNTIL ELIJAH COMES

The story of how the "return of Elijah" prophecy (see Isa. 42, Mal. 4) was actually fulfilled can be found in two separate places in the New Testament. It can also be found in a 1,900-year-old, non-biblical, Christian book that provides us with what is probably the most graphic example illustrating the importance of this prophecy.

What the Jews Expected About the Messiah

Justin Martyr was a very prominent Christian at a time when Christianity was still in its infancy. In *Eerdman's Handbook to the History of Christianity*, Justin Martyr is described as "the most notable of the second century [Christian] apologists."[1]

Justin Martyr lived in approximately A.D. 100. He wrote a book titled *The Dialogue with Trypho the Jew*. This book is a record of a discussion between Justin Martyr and Trypho—a Jewish rabbi. This "dialogue" begins with Justin telling the rabbi that he believes Jesus was the long-awaited Messiah. The following excerpt contains this rabbi's response.

It reads:

> When I (Justin) had said this, [the students who were with the rabbi] laughed; but he smiling, says, "I approve of your

other remarks, and admire the eagerness with which you study divine things; but it were better for you abide in the philosophy of Plato...."

Before Justin became a Christian, he was a follower of the Greek philosophers, and he still wore the characteristic flowing robes of a Roman philosopher. The quote continues:

"...It were better for you abide in the philosophy of Plato rather than be deceived by false words, and follow the opinions of people of no reputation...for when you have forsaken God, and reposed confidence in man, what safety still awaits you?"

Now, here's the important part:

"...But Christ—if he has indeed been born, and exists anywhere...has no power until Elijah comes to anoint him, and make him manifest to all. And you, having accepted a groundless report, invent a Christ for yourselves, and for his sake are inconsiderately perishing."[2]

In this one short passage, this rabbi reveals exactly what the Jewish religious leaders and the Jewish people of 2,000 years ago were expecting to see before the Messiah appeared. Trypho knew that Jesus could not possibly have been the Messiah because he knew from the unmistakable text of the "return of Elijah" prophecy that anyone who claimed to be the Christ before Elijah the Prophet had visibly returned from Heaven would have to be a false prophet.

This prophecy was one of the primary reasons why the Jewish people rejected Jesus' claims to be the Messiah. No one had seen Elijah return from Heaven yet, so how could Jesus possibly have been the Messiah?

"I Will Send You Elijah..."

Two thousand years ago, the Jewish people were expecting to see Elijah literally, physically descend from Heaven, possibly in the exact same chariot of fire that he had used to ascend into Heaven. Furthermore, they also expected that soon after Elijah's return, the Messiah was going to appear. And they knew that when the Messiah came, he not only was going to free them from Roman domination, but he also was going to exalt Israel over all the nations of the Earth. The Jewish people had good reason to believe these things. These expectations are derived from explicit statements made in the Bible. Jesus explains how these prophecies were actually fulfilled.

According to the Old Testament account, about 850 B.C., Elijah the prophet ascended into Heaven (see 2 Kings 2). Then, about 400 years later (in about 450 B.C.) the prophet Malachi promised that Elijah would return from Heaven before the Christ appears.

Malachi's prophecy reads:

> *Try me in this, says the Lord of Hosts: shall I not open for you the floodgates of heaven, to pour down a blessing upon you without measure...Lo, I will send you Elia* (Elijah), *the prophet before the day of the Lord comes, the great and terrible day* (Malachi 3:10, 4:5 Catholic Douay Bible)

Elijah Already Has Come

The Jewish religious leaders of Jesus' day were well aware of the "return of Elijah" prophecy. At one time, the rabbis had asked Jesus' disciples to explain how Jesus could possibly have been the Messiah when it was obvious that Elijah had not returned from Heaven yet.

The apostles couldn't answer this question, so they asked Jesus, "Why do the Jewish leaders insist Elijah must return before the Messiah comes?"

Jesus answered by first affirming that this question was valid and that this prophecy indeed was true. He said: *"They are right. Elijah must come and set everything in order...."* But then, to everyone's surprise, Jesus explained:

> *In fact, **he** [Elijah] **already has come, but he wasn't recognized**, and was badly mistreated by many.... Then the disciples realized he was speaking of **John the Baptist*** (Matthew 17:10-13 Living Bible Catholic Edition).

This account can also be found in Mark 9:11-13.

Clearly, Jesus taught that this was a true prophecy. Jesus agreed that Elijah indeed *"must return before the Messiah comes."* But then, to the surprise to everyone there, Jesus claimed that John the Baptist was the fulfillment of this prophecy.

This was one of the primary reasons that the entire nation of Israel did not accept the Messiah when He came the first time. Their understanding of what would happen when the Messiah would come was different than what actually happened. They believed that Elijah would come in a flaming chariot, the same way he left the Earth. After Elijah's return, then they believed the Messiah would come as a conquering king and would destroy all of Israel's enemies and rule and reign on the Earth forever. When Jesus came as a humble servant without much pomp and circumstance, they assumed that He was not the Messiah. As usual, people's thoughts and beliefs became more important than what God was actually doing.

Our relationship with God cannot be based on our preconceived notions about God. As believers we must open our hearts to God and allow Him to operate as He wants to operate. Whenever we attempt to dictate to God how He should do business, we miss out on the great things He is doing. Think about the irony in the fact that the religious leaders in the day of Jesus, whose job was to bring Israel into a close, personal relationship with God, wanted to kill the very God whom they claimed they were serving.

This happens when we get too much pride in ourselves. When we are more religious than in love with God, we miss God every time. That is why we must learn to obey God with open hearts and minds. We must seek God rather than try to dictate to God how He should operate. Obedience comes first and then revelation from God follows. If the Pharisees had sincerely sought after God with all their hearts, they would have received the Messiah when He first came. His Word is true completely and eternally.

John the Baptist

John was reluctant to baptize Jesus, for he said, *"I have need to be baptized by You"* (see Matt. 3:14). John knew that Jesus was the Son of God. Jesus had no need to be forgiven of sins because He was sinless. Knowing John's reluctance, Jesus told him, *"It is proper for us to do this to fulfill all righteousness."* So John obeyed Jesus and baptized him in the Jordan River.

> *And now also the axe is laid unto the root of the trees: therefore every tree which bringeth not forth good fruit is hewn down, and cast into the fire. I indeed baptize you with water unto repentance: But He that cometh after me is mightier than I, whose shoes I am not worthy to bear: He shall baptize you with the Holy Ghost, and with fire: Whose fan is in His hand, and He will throughly purge His floor, and gather His wheat into the garner; but He will burn up the chaff with unquenchable fire. Then cometh Jesus from Galilee to Jordan unto John, to be baptized of him. But John forbad him, saying, I have need to be baptized of Thee, and comest Thou to me? And Jesus answering said unto him, Suffer it to be so now: for thus it becometh us to fulfil all righteousness. Then he suffered Him. And Jesus, when He was baptized, went up straightway out of the water: and, lo, the heavens were opened unto Him, and He*

saw the Spirit of God descending like a dove, and lighting upon him: And lo a voice from heaven, saying, This is My beloved Son, in whom I am well pleased (Matthew 3:10-17).

Jesus was telling John that because he walked in the spirit of Elijah, he had to anoint Jesus so He could walk in the ministry of being the Christ. John, of course, knew who Jesus was. That is why John thought it absurd to think that he was supposed to baptize Jesus. He knew that Jesus was the divine Son of God who was holy and perfect. The tradition of baptism was done to ceremonially cleanse believers of their sins. Because John taught repentance from sin, those receiving the message felt a need to be baptized. We know that Jesus never sinned, nor did He have a sin nature because He was perfect and holy. Jesus was, however, acknowledging that He had to fulfill the prophecy that stated that Elijah had to anoint the Messiah.

God honors His Word above everything. Once God gives a Word, He submits Himself to that Word to guarantee that it comes to pass. God cannot go against His own Word, nor can He break His prophetic promises. Numbers 23:19 lets us know that God cannot lie, and when He says something, He has to perform it.

And He answered and told them, Elias verily cometh first, and restoreth all things; and how it is written of the Son of man, that He must suffer many things, and be set at nought (Mark 9:12).

The Transfiguration

And Jesus was saying to them, "Truly I say to you, there are some of those who are standing here who will not taste death until they see the kingdom of God after it has come with power." Six days later, Jesus took with Him Peter and James and John, and brought them up on a high mountain by themselves. And He was transfigured before them; and His garments became radiant and exceedingly white, as no launderer on earth can whiten them. Elijah appeared to them along with Moses; and they were talking with Jesus. Peter said to Jesus, "Rabbi, it is good for us to be here; let us make three tabernacles, one for You, and one for Moses, and one for Elijah." For he did not know what to answer; for they became terrified. Then a cloud formed, overshadowing them, and a voice came out of the cloud, "This is My beloved Son, listen to Him!" All at once they looked around and saw no one with them anymore, except Jesus alone. As they were coming down from the mountain, He gave them orders not to relate to anyone what they had seen, until the Son of Man rose from the dead. They seized upon that statement, discussing with one another what rising from the dead meant (Mark 9:1-10 NASB).

Here we see the demonstration of Malachi 4: Moses and Elijah are both on the mountain, and then they both dissolve and only Jesus the Christ is remaining. God wants us to know without any doubt that the Law is only a shadow of the Messiah. The Law lets us see God's nature and how He operates, but ultimately only by our faith in the Messiah can we really see the glory of God.

Moses represents the Law of God, the Law that brings success and peace to God's people. The Law causes us to demonstrate the nature and character of God in the Earth. Elijah represents turning back to the Torah. Because God's people seem to drift away from the Torah over and over again, God must release the spirit of Elijah to restore the Torah. Elijah prepares us for God's glory by showing us the way back to God.

As it did on the Mount of Transfiguration, at some point the Law will dissolve. When Jesus comes back for good, we will all be like Him. When that happens, Jesus will be the One who teaches us the Torah forever. Elijah will not be needed because no one will think to turn away. We will all become one with Him at the marriage supper of the Lamb. Elijah prepares us for that. After all is said and done, Jesus is all we will ever need. He is the fulfillment of all things, and therefore, when everything else fails, only Jesus will stand forever in eternity.

The question is, will you be standing with Him?

This book has not sought to make you believe that you are saved by the Law, which would be legalism. It is through the Law that we draw closer to Jesus. It is through walking in Torah that we honor God with our success and prosperity. Walking in agreement with the Father gives us power! Through walking in obedience to God's Word, we honor Him by being living epistles written by the hand of God. We glorify the Father when our obedience instills His shalom to the nations.

As stated in the opening pages of this book, the first Church moved in the power and authority that Jesus Christ meant for us to have. He gave His disciples an indication of what was to come before He ascended into Heaven.

> *And, being assembled together with them, commanded them that they should not depart from Jerusalem, but wait for the promise of the Father, which, saith He, ye have heard of Me. For John truly baptized with water; but ye shall be baptized with the Holy Ghost not many days hence. When they therefore were come together, they asked of Him, saying, Lord, wilt Thou at this time restore again the kingdom to Israel? And He said unto them, It is not for you to know the times or the seasons, which the Father hath put in His own power. But ye shall receive power, after that the Holy Ghost is come upon you: and ye shall be witnesses unto Me both in Jerusalem, and in all Judaea, and in Samaria, and unto the uttermost part of the earth* (Acts 1:4-8).

Jesus promised that those who will follow Him will walk in power and authority. The first Church demonstrated that for centuries. Even in the midst of persecution, they prospered. As I have demonstrated, when the power of God is moving in its fullest, satan cannot compete. As in the Garden of Eden and throughout history, his most effective weapon is subtlety and distortion, which he uses to weaken the move of the power of God. If he can change or pervert what God has put in place then God's people lose their effectiveness.

As in the Book of Daniel, the antichrist is able to overcome God's people by changing "times" and "laws." We have seen that he changes God's Word by subtly distorting the original meanings and intent of the Word. He also has been successful in changing the "times" or "seasons" of God. He accomplished this by replacing the original "appointed times" or "seasons" of God with holidays rooted in paganism. Jesus stated in the Book of Mark that the traditions of people make God's work of no effect (void) (see Mark 7:13). The proof of this is that the vast majority of the Church in America passionately observe Christmas and Easter while forsaking the Lord's feast days (appointed times) that He has commanded to *"keep it a feast [appointed time] by an ordinance for ever"* (Exod. 12:14). It is quite obvious that we have become much more passionate about human-made observances than the appointments that God has set. When was the last day they shut down New York City for a Passover celebration?

If the Book of Daniel is correct and the antichrist has used this subtle strategy to overcome God's people, then now is the time to get our power back!

Chapter 29

REVIVAL IN THE HOUSE OF GOD

A REPEATING PATTERN

Throughout Israel's history, we have seen a pattern that continued to repeat itself. This pattern is playing itself out today in the Church in America. Israel would be blessed; they would begin to compromise and fall in love with the world. Their love with affair with the world would cause them to turn away from God. God would send a prophet to show them their turning away. If they listened and repented, they were OK. Most of the time they would not heed the warnings of the prophets, and God would allow judgment to befall them. God would then raise up a righteous leader who would turn His people back to Him. Once again, Israel would return to the blessings of the Lord.

King Josiah, Nehemiah, and King Jehoshaphat were three leaders in Israel who turned the people's hearts back to God. These leaders compelled the people to rely on the Word of God and to follow His commandments. Israel was a great nation whenever they walked in the Torah of the Lord. When they turned away, God turned away from them.

The Bride Preparing for the Bridegroom

In this season, instead of one person, God is raising up a generation of prophets who are urging God's people to turn back to God. There is a prophetic call on the Church to turn His people back to the Torah so that we can return to the blessing and the power that God expects us to walk in. The spirit of Elijah is being released, and all who heed the call will walk in the power and the spirit of Elijah—the same Elijah who called fire down from Heaven, outran a chariot, and was whisked into Heaven on a flaming chariot. You can walk in the same power and anointing that he did.

"Can two walk together, except they be agreed?" (Amos 3:3). God wants us to walk in unity with Him in order to fulfill all things. Jesus is coming back again in response to His Bride beckoning His return. We are preparing for the eternal meeting with the Lamb of God, Jesus Christ. We as the true Church must have a sense of urgency in preparing the Bride for the Bridegroom. We have to look to remove the spots and blemishes that have corrupted the Church of Jesus Christ. Jesus died to reconnect us to Himself. He gives us the resurrection, and He is coming back to claim His beautiful Bride, the Church, the called out ones whose only desire is to spend eternity with the Bridegroom.

> *And, behold, I come quickly; and My reward is with Me, to give every man according as his work shall be. I am Alpha and Omega, the beginning and the end, the first and the last. Blessed are they that do His commandments that they may have right to the tree of life, and may enter in through the gates into the city. For without are dogs, and sorcerers, and whoremongers, and murderers, and idolaters, and whosoever loveth and maketh a lie. I Jesus have sent Mine angel to testify unto you these things in the churches. I am the root and the offspring of David, and the bright and morning star. And the Spirit and the bride say, Come. And let him that heareth say, Come. And let him that is athirst come. And whosoever will, let him take the water of life freely. For I testify unto every man that*

heareth the words of the prophecy of this book, If any man shall add unto these things, God shall add unto him the plagues that are written in this book: And if any man shall take away from the words of the book of this prophecy, God shall take away his part out of the book of life, and out of the holy city, and from the things which are written in this book. He which testifieth these things saith, Surely I come quickly. Amen. Even so, come, Lord Jesus. The grace of our Lord Jesus Christ be with you all. Amen (Revelation 22:12-21).

CONCLUSION

We are living in some perilous times. The Church in America is in disarray. The statistics of divorce in the Church are the same as the world.[1] Many people have turned away from the sound doctrine of the Bible. The New Age movement is gaining momentum, and even large parts of the Church have been deceived into following these false doctrines. We have truly done the thing that the Lord has warned His people not to do since the beginning of time; God has told us not to take on the ways of this world because it causes our hearts to turn away from Him.

God is looking for agreement with Him; only through being in sync with God do we truly walk in the authority that Jesus promised. In the Book of Acts, the Bible tells us that not only were the disciples in one place, but they were also in one accord (see Acts 2). It was this agreement with God and with each other that caused the Holy Spirit to burst into the Earth like a freight train. The disciples were all observing the feast of Pentecost when this happened. They were in one place in one accord.

Jesus prayed in the Book of John chapter 17 that all those who belong to the Lord become "one" as Jesus and the Father are "one." The concept of *oneness* ('echad) in the Hebraic way of thinking is what we would call unity. Unity comes through agreeing with God and being obedient to His ways and His timing. Jesus reiterated that by stating that He only said what the Father said and did what the Father did. This is total agreement between Jesus and the Father.

The interesting thing about unity is that all parties must have the same information in order to be unified. An army platoon all must get the exact same instructions at the same time in order to march in unison. When that happens, there is nothing more powerful than an army marching in unison. A unified army is one that is hard to beat.

We are the army of God. We are in a war with the devil. God gives us His Spirit and His Word to equip us for battle. When we are in unison we *cannot* lose! Jesus said that the gates of hell *will not* prevail against the Church that He died for (see Matt. 16:18).

Jesus is coming back very soon, and when He does, He is looking for those who will be in unison with Him. They will be in sync with Him, walking beside Him in victory. He has given us His true Word, the one that contains the battle plan of the Kingdom of God. He has given us the appointed times that teach us how the Lord operates and what His timing is. That is why the devil has always tried to disrupt the battle plan for God's people.

Without a doubt, we have salvation through the gift of grace. That grace only comes through faith in Jesus our Lord and Savior. It is on the cross of Calvary that Jesus won the battle against satan to give us eternal life. We are saved by faith and not by works, as the Bible says (see Gal. 2:16). However, there is another element in God. There is much more to being a child of God than just going to Heaven. When we search the heart of God and learn more of His Word and His ways, then we are empowered to bring forth the Kingdom of God with power. God didn't just save us to wait to go to Heaven; He also empowers us to bring Heaven here on the Earth.

The question is, will you be ready?

This book is not meant to condemn, but to encourage—building up and not tearing down. I love the Church that Jesus died for. I want nothing more than for us to share the same authority together like the first apostles did. That is why God gave me this book, to expose the devices of the devil so that we can walk in truth and victory and not deception and defeat, to go deeper in the Lord than any of us thought was possible.

I want to challenge you to take a step of faith. Turn away from complacency, religion, and tradition to become the true ecclesia, the Church of Jesus, who is called the Christ, the son of the living God!

ENDNOTES

CHAPTER 1

1. *Strong's Concordance with Hebrew and Greek Lexicon,* Greek # 1411.

2. "Correspondence Between Pliny and the Emperor Trajan Pliny," translated by William Melmoth (revised by F. C. T. Bosanquet).

3. *The Apology of Tertullian,* translated and annotated by Wm. Reeve, A.M. Sometime Vicar of Cranford, Middlesex; and *The Meditations of the Emperor Marcus Aurelius Antonius,* translated by Jeremy Collier, A.M. Griffith, Farran, Okeden & Welsh (Newberry House London & Sydney); *The Ancient & Modern Library of Theological Literature, vol. 31.*

4. Dr. Robert Heidler, *The Messianic Church Arising* (Glory of Zion International Ministries, 2006), 18.

5. Phillip Schaff, *History of the Christian Church,* Chapter 1, "The Spread of Christianity" (Hendrickson Publishers, 2006).

6. *Ibid.*

CHAPTER 2

1. *Strong's Concordance with Hebrew and Greek Lexicon,* Hebrew # 1881.

CHAPTER 3

1. Even-Shoshan, A., *The New Dictionary: Complete Treasury of the Hebrew Language*, Kiryat Sefer, Jerusalem (1983), In Hebrew (item 4 is Hebrew citation).

CHAPTER 5

1. *The American Heritage® Dictionary of the English Language,* Fourth Edition copyright ©2000 by Houghton Mifflin Company. Updated in 2009.
2. *Strong's Concordance with Hebrew and Greek Lexicon,* Greek # 1461.

CHAPTER 6

1. *Strong's Exhaustive Concordance,* Hebrew #3259.
2. *Ibid.,* Hebrew #770.

CHAPTER 8

1. *Strong's Concordance with Hebrew and Greek Lexicon,* Hebrew # 1263.

CHAPTER 9

1. Eusebius, *Life of Constantine,* Book 3, Chapter XVII, Constantine's letter to the churches.

CHAPTER 10

1. William L. Shirer, *The Rise and Fall of the Third Reich* (New York: Simon & Schuster, 1990).
2. *Ibid.*
3. *Ibid.*
4. Martin Luther, "Luther to George Spalatin," quoted in *Luther's Correspondence and Other Contemporaneous Letters,* trans. Henry

Preserved Smith (Philadelphia: Lutheran Publication Society, 1913), 1:29.

5. *Weimar Ausgabe* 51:194-196; J.G. Walch, *Dr. Martin Luthers Sämmtliche Schriften,* 23 vols. (St. Louis: Concordia, 1883), 12:1264-1267.

CHAPTER 11

1. Strong's Concordance with Hebrew and Greek Lexicon, *Hebrew # 7935.*

CHAPTER 13

1. *Strong's Concordance with Hebrew and Greek Lexicon*, Hebrew # 4150.

2. Anthony Kemp, *Witchcraft and Paganism Today* (London: Michael O'Mara, 1993), 3.

CHAPTER 14

1. World Book Encyclopedia, *Vol. 3,* (Chicago, IL: World Book Inc., 1986), 408; The Catholic Encyclopedia, R.C. Broderick, ed. (Milwaukee, WI: 1975); Ronald Knox, *The Mass In Slow Motion* (New York: Sheed & Ward, Inc., 1948).

2. "Pagan Origins," *History of the Christmas Tree,* http://www.christmastreehistory.net/pagan (accessed March 14, 2011); "Origins of Christmas," video, *The History Channel,* http://www.history.com/videos/history-of-christmas (accessed March 14, 2011); Mike Nichols, "Midwinter Night's Eve: Yule," *The Wiccan/Pagan Times,* http://www.twpt.com/yule.htm (accessed March 14, 2011).

3. Robert K. Barnhart, *The Barnhart Concise Dictionary of Etymology* (1995); Joseph Bosworth and T. Northcote Toller, *An Anglo-Saxon Dictionary* (Oxford: Oxford University Press, 1898).

4. http://www.therefinersfire.org/antisemitism_in_church.htm

5. Francis X. Weiser, *Handbook of Christian Feasts and Customs* (New York: Harcourt, Brace, and World, 1958).

6. John Matthews and Caitlin Matthews, *The Winter Solstice: The Sacred Traditions of Christmas* (Wheaton, IL: Quest Books, 1998).

CHAPTER 15

1. http://www.history.com

CHAPTER 16

1. Strong's Concordance with Hebrew and Greek Lexicon.

2. Billy Graham, *Storm Warning* (Thomas Nelson, 2010), 78-79.

3. Strong's Concordance with Hebrew and Greek Lexicon, Greek # 2315.

4. Strong's Concordance with Hebrew and Greek Lexicon, Greek # 5342.

CHAPTER 18

1. Ian Wilson, *The Bible Is History* (Washington, D.C.: Regnery Publishing, Inc, 2000), 205. Emphasis added by the author.

2. Montgomery, HC, 26.

3. F.E. Peters, HH, 50.

4. Geisler, GIB, 385.

5. Leach, OB, 145.

6. Sir Fredrick Kenyon, *The Bible & Archaeology* (New York: Harper & Row, 1940), 288.

7. Dockery, Matthews, and Sloan, FBI, 176.

8. *Ibid,* 182.

9. Sir Frederic Kenyon, The Bible & Archaeology.

CHAPTER 20

1. Frederick Fyvie Bruce, *History of the Bible in English* (Cambridge: Lutterworth, 2002).

2. David Otis Fuller, *Which Bible?* (Institute for Biblical Textual Studies, 1997).

CHAPTER 21

1. J. Gordon Melton, "New Age Transformed," *Institute for the Study of American Religion,* http://web.archive.org/web/20060614001357 /religiousmovements.lib.virginia.edu/nrms/newage.html (accessed March 14, 2011).

2. Elena Petrovna Blavatskaja (1888), *The Secret Doctrine,* (Theosophy Foundation of Georgia, Theosophical Publication Co), Online Computer Llibrary Center61915001.

3. J. Gordon Melton, Jerome Clark, and Aidan A. Kelly, editors, *New Age Almanac* (Detroit, MI: Gale Research Inc., 1991), 16.

4. Robert S. Ellwood and Harry B. Partin, *Religious and Spiritual Groups in Modern America* (Englewood Cliffs, NJ: Prentice Hall, 1988), 63, 79-80.

5. James A. Santucci, quoted in *Dictionary of Gnosis & Western Esotericism.*

6. http://www.theosociety.org/etgloss/etg-hp.htm

7. Life and Letters of Brooke Foss Westcott (London: Macmillan and Co., 1903), Vol. I, pp. 73-74; The Gospel According to St. John (1881; rpt. Grand Rapids: Wm. B. Eerdmans Publishing Company, 1971)

8. Life and Letters of Fenton John Anthony Hort (1896); Brooke Foss Westcott, quoted in Venn, J. & J.A., Alumni Cantabrigienses, Cambridge University Press, 10 vols, 1922–1958.

9. Brooke Foss Westcott, quoted in Venn, J. & J.A., Alumni Cantabrigienses, Cambridge University Press, 10 vols, 1922–1958.

10. K.W. Clark, http://www.wayoflife.org/database/westcotthort.html

11. E.C. Colwell, http://www.wayoflife.org/database/westcotthort.html

12. Zane Hodges, http://www.wayoflife.org/database/westcotthort.html

13. Alfred Martin, http://www.graceway.com/articles/article_025.html

CHAPTER 22

1. http://www.virginiamollenkott.com/

2. http://www.youtube.com/xsgtusmc, This is a live recording of Dr. Logsdon renouncing the NASV Bible.

CHAPTER 24

1. *Strong's Exhaustive Concordance*, Hebrew #7725.

CHAPTER 25

1. *Strong's Exhaustive Concordance*, Greek # 1515, Hebrew #7999.

CHAPTER 26

1. *Strong's Exhaustive Concordance*, Hebrew # 8451, 3384.

2. *Strong's Exhaustive Concordance*, Hebrew #6743.

CHAPTER 28

1. *Eerdman's Handbook to the History of Christianity*, Tim Dowley, ed., (Grand Rapids, MI: Eerdman's Publishing Company, 1977), 108.

2. *The Ante Nicene Fathers, Volume 1: Apostolic Fathers, Justin Martyr, Inrenaeus,* (Peabody, MA: Hendrickson Publishers, 1994), 198.

CONCLUSION

1. Barna Research Group. http://www.barna.org/barna-update /article/15-familykids/42-new-marriage-and-divorce-statistics-released

SOURCES

1. G.A. Riplinger, *New Age Bible Versions*, 1993.

2. Episcopal, witness, June 1991.

3. *The Catholic Encyclopedia,* R.C. Broderick, 1975 ed., Nihil Obstat, Richard J. Sklba, Censor Librorum. Imprimatur, Archbishop William E. Cousins, Milwaukee, WI.

4. Ronald Knox, *The Mass In Slow Motion*, 1948, Sheed & Ward, Inc., New York, NY. Nihil Obstat, E.C. Messenger, Censor Deputatus. Imprimatur, E. Morrogh Bernard, Vic. Gen.

5. David J. Meyer, *The True Meaning Of Christ-Mass.*

6. http://www.catanna.com/paganholidays.htm

7. http://www.ecauldron.com/holidays.php

8. http://www.therefinersfire.org/feasts2.htm

9. The Good News: July/August 2004.

10. *The Case for Christ*, Lee Strobel, Zondervan Publishing, 1998

11. Josh McDowell, *The Evidence for Christianity*, Nelson Publishing, 2006.

12. www.religioustolerance.org/gl_c.htm

13. www.reformationonline.com/glossary.htm

14. Dutch Sheets, *Authority in Prayer*, Bethany House, 2006.

15. Michael Rood, *Biblical Hebrew Calendar*, 2006.

16. Robert D. Heidler, *Cycles of God, God's Key to Increase and Blessing*, Glory of Zion International Ministries.

17. Robert D. Heidler, *The Messianic Church Arising*, Glory of Zion International Ministries, 2006.

18. Carol Wallace, Lifeline Ministies, P.O. Box 15503, Harrisburg, PA 17105.

19. www.jewishmag.com

20. Philip Schaff, *History of the Christian Church.*

21. Pierre Allix, *Ecclesiastical History of Ancient Churches of the Albigenses*, published in Oxford at the Clarendon Press in 1821.

More About Joseph L. Green

Contact information
Pastor Joseph L Green
Head Pastor, Antioch Assembly
646 Graham Street, Harrisburg, Pa. 17110

Email: antiochpastors@gmail.com
Facebook: Joseph L Green Jr.
Twitter: @jgministries
Youtube: joegreen720

Other Books by Joseph L. Green

From Kilos to the Kingdom

IN THE RIGHT HANDS, THIS BOOK WILL CHANGE LIVES!

Most of the people who need this message will not be looking for this book. To change their lives, you need to put a copy of this book in their hands.

> *But others (seeds) fell into good ground, and brought forth fruit, some a hundred-fold, some sixty-fold, some thirty-fold* (Matthew 13:8).

Our ministry is constantly seeking methods to find the good ground, the people who need this anointed message to change their lives. Will you help us reach these people?

> *Remember this—a farmer who plants only a few seeds will get a small crop. But the one who plants generously will get a generous crop* (2 Corinthians 9:6).

EXTEND THIS MINISTRY BY SOWING
3 BOOKS, 5 BOOKS, 10 BOOKS, OR MORE TODAY,
AND BECOME A LIFE CHANGER!

Thank you,

Don Nori Sr., Founder
Destiny Image
Since 1982